An Illustrated Guide to Tactical Diagramming

An Illustrated Guide to Tactical Diagramming

SID HEAL

Lantern Books • New York

A Division of Booklight Inc.

2006
Lantern Books
One Union Square West, Suite 201
New York, NY 10003

Printed in the United States

green press
INITIATIVE

Lantern Books has elected to print this title on Natures Natural a 30% post-consumer recycled paper, processed chlorine-free. As a result, we have saved the following resources:

4 Trees (40' tall and 6-8" diameter)
1,777 Gallons of Wastewater
1 million BTU's of Total Energy
113 Pounds of Solid Waste
394 Pounds of Greenhouse Gases

As part of Lantern Books' commitment to the environment we have joined the Green Press Initiative, a nonprofit organization supporting publishers in using fiber that is not sourced from ancient or endangered forests. We hope that you, the reader, will support Lantern and the Green Press Initiative in our endeavor to preserve the ancient forests and the natural systems on which all life depends. One way is to buy books that cost a little more but make a positive commitment to the environment not only in their words, but in the paper that they were published on. For more information, visit www.greenpressinitiative.org

Environmental impact estimates were made using the Environmental Defense Paper Calculator. For more information visit: www.papercalculator.org.

FSC
www.fsc.org
MIX
Paper from
responsible sources
FSC® C013483

"A house is built of walls and beams;
a home is built with love and dreams."

To the builder of our home, Linda, my bride of 40 years.

Table of Contents

Acknowledgements. ix

Preface. xiii

Chapter One: Introduction to Tactical Digramming 1

Chapter Two: Terrain Analysis 9

Chapter Three: The Urban Landscape 23

Chapter Four: Housing Trends. 37

Chapter Five: Building Principles 51

Chapter Six: Roofs 63

Chapter Seven: Vents and Ducts 79

Chapter Eight: Doors 93

Chapter Nine: Windows 105

Chapter Ten: Rooms. 125

Chapter Eleven: Extra Rooms, Upper Stories and Multiple Dwellings. . . 143

Chapter Twelve: Saved Rounds 159

Appendix A: Concept Glossary 177

Appendix B: Diagramming Principles (Rules of Thumb) 183

Appendix C: Useful Websites 187

Appendix D: Tactical Diagramming—Step by Step 193

Index 197

Acknowledgements

As with all books, but especially reference books, the thoughts and words of the author are merely reflections of his mentors. This book is no exception. Consequently, it is important to recognize their contribution, but especially so in this case, since they are nearly all my family!

Like many young boys, I first learned the basics of construction at the hands of my father. One of my earliest birthday gifts was a small hammer, a pound of drywall nails and a few scraps of pine into which I promptly pounded every nail. I then pounded most of them back out and renailed them. I repeated this process until I could no longer pull the nails out or they were too bent to reuse. A most inauspicious beginning to be sure, but such was my love of construction that it remains in my memory today. My father and I, Charles Gene Heal, share the same first name but for no discernible reason have always been known by our middle names. Likewise, we share many of the same interests, not the least of which has been a feeling of deep personal satisfaction from building something. While my dad never had a construction license, he farmed at least part time his entire working life, and, as for all farmers, construction was an essential job skill. Many of my fondest memories are watching and helping him build sheds, garages, barns, chicken coops, porches, and, as my five brothers and sisters arrived, the room addition that is still part of a house that must be more than 100 years old.

Likewise, many of the things I learned at his knee had applications far beyond the context in which I learned them, even in resolving the tactical interventions that have become the focus of my own career. "Measure twice—cut once" emphasizes the necessity of accuracy in the information we rely on to make irreversible decisions. "A poor craftsman blames his tools" identifies not only the importance of craftsmanship but the responsibility we must accept for our own actions. In retrospect, the lives my father was shaping and building were far more lasting and important than the things we were constructing.

On a farm, every project is a family project, and in the same manner my two younger brothers, Chris and Brad, were as much a part of this maturation process and developed the same love for fixing and building things. Both are licensed builders with their own companies, but while Chris has always wanted to work with wood, Brad's first love was mechanics. Joined later by my nephew Mike (Chris's son), who upon graduation from high school promptly enrolled in college and obtained his builder's license while barely out of his teens, have reviewed this text for accuracy, insight and just plain common sense. Over the years we've had innumerable conversations on construction techniques, practices and laws for reasons as trivial as my simple curiosity and as critical as planning a high-risk warrant, and eventually ensuring the accuracy of this text.

My natural proclivity for building provided me with an abundance of employment opportunities as I attended college, not the least of which was for my future father-in-law, Orville Wagner. Wagner Steel, Inc. was started as a blacksmith's shop many years before my wife and I were born but had long since evolved into a premier shop for structural steel and custom metal work when I started in 1970. If there was ever a craftsman in steel and iron it was my father-in-law, who could use a hammer, forge and anvil to create realistic bark, stems, leaves and flowers in red-hot steel and iron. While most of the construction was for retail and small businesses, homeowners would often use steel to span spaces not possible with wood, and I learned about loads, gussets, bracing and other structural techniques. Like the lessons I learned from my own father, however, the greatest and most enduring lessons I learned were only generally related to construction.

Last, but certainly not least, is one of my close friends in the Los Angeles Sheriff's Department, Lt. Chris Branuelas. While the origins of this text can be traced back to the mid 1980s when I was planning high-risk warrants on an almost daily basis, I had always longed to do a more comprehensive book on the subject. Upon returning from Operation Iraqi Freedom in the fall of 2003, I set about in earnest to finishing the work I'd begun decades before. It was soon painfully apparent, however, that this book would require substantial illustrations to be even minimally comprehensible. My skills as an artist were not only meager, they were missing altogether! It was in a casual conversation that Chris volunteered to help and succeeded beyond my wildest expectations. The degree to which the reader is capable of visualizing these concepts can be attributed entirely to him.

Preface

Somewhere in the midst of my sophomore year of high school it became apparent, even to me, that academics were not my forte. To be sure, it wasn't for lack of effort on the part of my teachers, or even lack of intellect of my own; I simply lacked the most indispensable prerequisite for success—motivation. The academic standard to which I aspired was that amorphous, minimal threshold that would allow me to pass a course without having to actually study. In fact, I'm pretty sure that if I brought a schoolbook home at any time during my high school years my guardian angel has it written in his diary somewhere.

By my senior year the powers that be decided that if I were to succeed at anything in life I would require a trade, and I was one of about five boys assigned to a new educational concept called "co-op." While the proper name for the program has long since faded from memory, if I ever bothered learning it at all, the co-op project linked students who seemed genetically destined to work with their hands with skilled craftsmen. Thus I spent half a day, several days a week, throughout my senior year learning carpentry. I loved it! For the first time math made sense. I needed to use square feet to determine everything from the amount of flooring, siding and sheathing to the number of cement blocks in a basement wall. I needed to know how to figure out volumes for concrete floors and HVAC installations. I needed to know geometry for designing rafters and trusses. Government took on a whole new meaning with planning codes and zoning ordinances. Even social studies had a place as I learned why some things are built according to a custom even when not required by law. And so it was that I prepared for life in the construction industry. It was not to be, however.

As with many young men at the time, my life was forever reoriented by Vietnam. I guess I should have paid a little more attention to geography and current events. The U.S. Marines' battle at Khe Sanh raged in the spring of my senior year but passed by me nearly unnoticed. Places like Con Thien, Gio Linh, the Rockpile, Dong Ha, and Quang Tri were no more familiar to me than the French and Latin words I had to learn to pass English Literature. It never once crossed my mind that by the very next summer I would personally visit those places.

Upon my return from Vietnam the only two things of which I was absolutely certain was that I'd found my life's love in a girl I had met while en route to Vietnam, and that I wanted to go to college in the worst way. I promptly married the girl (Linda, my wife for the past 40 years) and enrolled in college (on academic probation). The motivation and determination were there this time, and within a few years I had both bachelor's and master's degrees. It wasn't until the mid 1980s that I returned to my studies in carpentry, albeit for an entirely different reason.

In my youthful farming days, the idea of becoming a police officer was never on my radar screen. By 1985, however, I was a sergeant with the Los Angeles Sheriff's Department assigned to our Special Enforcement Bureau. I was team leader of "Blue Team," one of the Department's six full-time SWAT teams. The Special Enforcement Bureau routinely handles about 200 incidents a year dealing with the worst of the worst. In more than 30 years of law enforcement, this was the only place where television actually resembled police work. I personally planned and participated in operations that involved snipers, terrorists, organized crime and street gangs, armed with scoped rifles, automatic assault weapons, belt-fed machine guns, IEDs[1] and shoulder-

---

1. Improvised Explosive Devices

fired, anti-armor rocket launchers. Just as interesting were their defensive fortifications, whether as simple as anchoring steel bars over doors and windows or as elaborate as hidden crawl spaces and escape routes, or even underground, concrete bunker complexes. It was here that my knowledge of carpentry and building practices again became useful.

Over the years I've taught a number of classes on tactical diagramming and worked with a number of teams in different regions and states in diagramming target locations for high-risk warrants and the like. I want to make it clear from the outset that I didn't invent it. The first time I heard about how outside architectural features might be used to predict interior floor plans was from my team scout, Ray Reyes, and his back-up, Abelardo "Abby" Marquez. Later, fellow SWAT members like Mike Connolly, Tommy Lambrecht and Mike LeFever, who also had an interest in construction, showed me some of the methods they'd already worked out. The epiphany came, however, during a fishing trip with my younger brother Chris in the Saginaw Bay area of Lake Huron. In the long, quiet hours waiting for the fish to bite, I mentioned our need to figure out how to determine floor plans from outside architectural features. Chris had already received his Michigan Builders License and owned his own construction company. In the following hours he described all the various building code requirements and construction practices that "standardized" the look, feel and shape of housing. It was then that I decided to go back and seriously study building construction.

Contractors in many states, including the one I live in (California) require applicants to have worked in the construction industry for a given number of years under the tutelage of other contractors and tradesmen in addition to passing a comprehensive written test covering both construction law and the building trades. By 1988 I had amassed the necessary years of apprenticeship because I had worked part-time with other contractors to put myself through college. Even after becoming a deputy sheriff I worked part-time to supplement my entry-level income.

(While I never really mastered mathematics, the difference between what I could make in construction and what I made in law enforcement was conspicuous and substantial.) I had been studying the building codes and building practices for several years because I was using them every day for tactical diagramming for SWAT operations, and so in 1988 I took and passed the California contractor's test and became a licensed general contractor.

Tactical diagramming is a science, a skill and an art. It is a science in that it uses knowledge of building codes and zoning ordinances, coupled with an understanding of sound building practices, to determine the nature, use and configuration of buildings. It is a skill in that a tactical diagrammer—even one without the familiarity of the building trades—who practices is more efficient and effective than one who does not. Finally, it is an art in that when the science and skill do not reliably reveal clues to confidently diagram a building, the intuition, imagination and ingenuity of the diagrammer must supplement.

Tactical diagramming is a technique, not a tactic or a strategy. It will not provide answers to tactical questions, but rather reveals those essential elements that contribute to a sound plan. An ability to "see" behind a wall, or know the configuration of an interior room by the way the door swings, can hardly be understated, especially if you are the one about to make entry and expect to encounter deadly force. As one of my young Marines[2] in Iraq once asked, "Sir? Do you survive all these encounters because you've done it so often that you know what to do and how to do it, or does God grant you just so many chances and when you use them up they're just gone?" Either way you answer that, you're better off knowing where the threat is and how best to counter it. It is with this in mind that this information is compiled and presented.

---

2. L/Cpl Glenn Hunter, somewhere north of the LOD near Rumaylah, Iraq, late March 2003

CHAPTER 1

Introduction to Tactical Diagramming

Did you ever wonder why you can climb a flight of stairs without looking where you step? Do you think about opening a door with one hand and turning on the lights with the other? What about which faucet handle is for the hot water and which is for the cold? Probably not—after all, why should you? The fact is, however, that you possess a vast amount of construction knowledge that you have unconsciously assimilated over the years. It docsn't matter that you can't tell a coping saw from a chain saw or that you have never successfully driven a nail. Surprised? You needn't be. People are creatures of habit. We don't like to go to a strange motel room and discover that the shower faucet handles were reversed and we are being doused with water straight from the Bering Sea. We want to walk up any stairway in any building, or even outside at a park, without once looking where we step. We even want to do it in darkness. We've come to expect it—even demand it!

Once you think about it, your knowledge of how buildings are constructed is really quite extensive. You seem to sense that when you exit a store or restaurant the exit door will push away from you, and when you enter your neighbor's house the door will open away from you and into the house. But let's carry this just a bit further. Let me see if I can describe your house. The only thing I need to know is approximately how old your house is. For sake of argument, let's say it's less than 20 years old and you live in an urban or suburban area. (After all, over 90 percent of us do![1]) Without knowing you or having ever seen your house, let's see how many features I can describe.

As I approach your house there is a sidewalk leading to your front door from either the driveway[2] or the sidewalk along your street.[3] You don't have a very large porch—in fact you quite likely don't have a porch at all! Instead there will be a small entryway.[4] When you greet me you will open the 3-foot-wide entrance door[5] toward you and into the house. As I step in, I will be standing in a small foyer near the living room. If you have a two-story house I can see the stairway leading to the upstairs bedrooms, and the foot of the staircase is only a few steps from where I am standing. The bedrooms are separated by either closets or a bathroom, and the interior doors swing into the rooms and against one of the walls. The light switches are on the inside wall of the rooms and on the doorknob side of the door but slightly higher.

As you begin to give me a tour, I notice that you have a sliding glass door entering onto a patio at the rear[6] and that the largest windows in the house are nearby. I also notice that your leisure activity "toys," like a pool, hot tub, swing set, hammock and the like, are in the back yard. The perimeter fence around your property is 6 feet tall and either a wooden slat fence or a cinderblock wall.[7] Your garage is attached to the house and there is a door leading into it from the

---

1. Paul B.Horton and Chester L. Hunt, *Sociology* (San Francisco: McGraw-Hill Book Company, 1968), p. 432. While this information seems dated, it remains reliable and consistent for present-day circumstances.
2. The driveway is at least 16 feet wide to allow for two cars to be parked side by side.
3. The sidewalk along the street is about 4 feet wide and immediately adjacent to the curb. In older parts of the city it will be only about 3 feet wide with a grassy area between the sidewalk and the curb.
4. The entryway is barely large enough to hold me, seldom larger than about 20 square feet.
5. To be precise, the door will be 36 inches wide, 80 inches tall and 1-3/4 inches thick.
6. If you have a more luxurious house, it might be a set of French doors that swing into your house.
7. If you live in a northern region, especially the Midwest, this fence might be a shorter chain-link fence or, in rarer cases, may not exist at all.

kitchen or family room. When I look at this door I notice that it has self-closing hinges.[8]

How am I doing? Chances are extremely good that a number of the features I described are applicable to your house. Let's try a few more. It's better than even that your house siding is either white or off-white with a darker, earth-tone trim and that all the bedrooms are next to each other. If you have a two-story house, they are all upstairs. If I stand at your kitchen sink I'm looking out a window and the refrigerator is slightly behind and to one side of me but within 6 feet.

To be sure, it is impossible to describe every attribute of a house I've never seen, but how many of the features are the same as your own house? If I called even half of them correctly, what do you think I could do if I could see some photographs of your house or walk by on the outside?

I was introduced to tactical diagramming very early in 1985 when I was assigned as a team leader to one of our six full-time SWAT teams at the Los Angeles Sheriff's Department. My scout, Ray Reyes, and back-up, Abelardo "Abby" Marquez, would take me on scouting missions and point out fortifications prepared by suspects, where they thought the suspects would be in the structure at the time of the warrant service, where the structure would be most vulnerable to breaching, and other critical tactical information. The fact that they were right so often made a believer out of me and I tried to master a technique that I could see would be invaluable in my new role in SWAT operations.

The bellwether event occurred later that year, however, when my team was assigned to serve a high-risk narcotics warrant in an affluent community about 25 miles east of Los Angeles proper. It seems that drug dealers, like other prosperous merchants, did not live where they sold their wares but rather in quite luxurious homes (by my own living standards) in neighborhoods where I'd have to put a lawnmower in my

---

8. Like the front (entrance) door, this door is also 80 inches tall and 1-3/4 inches thick (solid core—that is, without any dead spaces inside the door), but it will be only about 30 to 32 inches wide.

truck to avoid arousing suspicion if I drove through. Because money was not a serious problem, they also, quite naturally, spent it on reinforcing their structures and property to prevent intrusion, most often from other drug dealers. The fact that they were often able to do this without raising the suspicions of their innocent neighbors was a testament not only to their ingenuity but also to their craftsmanship.

This house was no exception. It was a beautiful two-story house with a professionally manicured lawn and a stone wall that enclosed a small courtyard around the front door. Aerial photographs revealed a pool in the back yard with a barbecue and patio. It was located on a cul-de-sac in a quiet neighborhood, and from all outside appearances it could have belonged to any well-to-do businessman. The affidavit of the search warrant revealed a far more sinister picture, however, as the house was listed as one of three "targets" in different parts of the county in which a drug cartel led by a ruthless kingpin used it as a warehouse distribution point to avoid having an entire cache of drugs in one location. Drug transactions would take place in nearby restaurants and then couriers would pick-up the required amount and type of drugs from the location and bring it to the sales site. The drugs were always guarded by at least two "gunslingers" who were known for being completely merciless and had a reputation for killing their rivals.

The warrant "work-up" began like every other I'd been involved with to that point, with surveillance and reconnaissance "drive-bys" and "fly-bys." The narcotic investigators were interviewed and provided photographs of suspects. The real insight came, however, when we interviewed a local SWAT team who had conducted their own operation on the same house the year before. One of the SWAT officers provided a notebook sketch of the inside of the house and mentioned that this would be the third warrant service on the location in the last two years, as yet another local SWAT team had hit the location some months prior. After we concluded the interview he said something in passing that saved our lives a few days later: "You know, the guy always fixes and reinforces where he's been hit in the past." We asked him what he meant and he said that the first SWAT team had used the front door of house for entry. A few weeks later they noted that the courtyard had been built surrounding the front door and served in effect to channel visitors into a "kill zone," and that the front door was now also barred. The second SWAT team had used a chain saw through the wooden garage door to gain entry, and he'd bet that there were now bars on the inside door from the garage to the house. In continuing the work-up we noted in our surveillance photographs that even seemingly inaccessible upstairs windows were barred. Not only was this particularly conspicuous when compared with neighboring houses, it provided a great deal of insight into the amount of resistance we might expect when we demanded entry to serve the warrant. The more successful drug dealers are prepared to destroy their merchandise in very quick order to avoid being caught with it. With the exception of all but the largest operations, only about 60 seconds is usually needed to destroy the evidence that would result in their incarceration.

As the plan evolved we decided to demand entry (as required by law) at the entrance door of the location, but be prepared to do an entry by pulling the bars from a second-story window over a small roof projection. From the officer's sketch we knew that the window serviced a small balcony on a staircase between the two stories. Forced entries are a risky business and a second-story "bar pull" entry is nearly unheard of, but because of our belief in the suspects' intentions and our knowledge of the floor plan we determined that, while not appealing, it presented the best means of gaining access to the interior of the house without confronting fortifications and armed guards.

The operation began as planned with a deputy at the entrance door pounding hard and demanding entry, albeit from behind the small, stone courtyard wall. He was immediately taken under fire as a suspect began firing a handgun out through the door and windows near the entrance door. The plan for forced entry was then implemented with a diversion to the rear sliding door and the second-story bars simultaneously pulled from the window. As the entry team gained access to the balcony a second suspect began firing an assault rifle at them. One of the team members returned fire, killing him. The first suspect firing out the front door then retreated farther back into the house, where he was subsequently captured without serious injury.

As you can imagine, the debriefing was lengthy and complex and involved not only SWAT members but narcotics, homicide and District Attorney investigators. As suspected, the inside garage door of our target had indeed been barred and would have trapped our entry team in the garage if we had tried to follow in the path of the previous SWAT team. One thing that was startlingly clear to everyone was that the knowledge of the floor plan of the location revealed the only feasible access point for the forced entry and our knowledge of how to exploit it had been a decisive factor in our survival. My interest in learning how to use architectural features to predict interior floor plans had moved from mild curiosity to fervid enthusiasm.

In the years that followed I have seen diagrams as simple as lines in the dirt or sketches in a notebook, and as elaborate as computerized, three-dimensional, virtual "walk throughs," complete with digital photographs of critical features like control panels, crawl spaces and emergency exits. We've used them to plan operations as simple as serving a search warrant and as complex as the 1994 World Cup Soccer Finals and the annual Tournament of Roses Parade. Regardless of the features and details, a tactical diagram is only as good as the information from which it is derived. To the best of my knowledge, this book is the first of its kind dealing specifically with this subject, but it is not intended to be exhaustive. Indeed, with the myriad of variations possible in construction materials and practices, I intentionally avoided as many of the "exceptions to the rule" as possible and stayed with the tried and true. While I am confident that the procedures, rules and principles described in this book will provide reasonably accurate and reliable tactical diagrams, differences in culture, climate and even personal taste must always be considered.

The subjects in this book are arranged to allow a novice tactical diagrammer to begin with a very broad perspective, such as conducting a terrain analysis and the characteristics that distinguish the urban landscape, before delving into the details of residential construction. Hopefully this will provide the reader with a foundation of knowledge so that the more detailed information provided later will make more sense. Diagramming principles and rules are italicized so that they are more readily identifiable. The book is heavily indexed and cross-referenced, and key concepts and principles are also provided as appendices so that a reader can quickly find the information being sought without undue labor. Additionally, twenty tried-and-true diagramming principles are provided as a "cheat sheet" in Appendix B to allow a tactical diagrammer to reliably predict floor plans without having to read the entire book.

CHAPTER 2

Terrain Analysis

It has long been recognized that terrain has a tremendous influence on how tactical operations are conducted. From as far back as prehistoric times our ancestors have used terrain to assist them in a hunt when they would drive game over a cliff or into deep water. In fact, because weapons were so primitive, the entire success of a hunt could depend upon how well the influence of terrain was understood and exploited. In the old West, cowboys would herd cattle into draws and canyons to make them easier to count or catch and brand. Military units still seek high ground to gain observation and broaden fields of fire. Terrain provides opportunities and/or imposes limitations, sometimes providing a decisive advantage to a commander who recognizes its significance and exploits it. In the same manner, proper evaluation and utilization of terrain will provide advantages for law enforcement operations.

While we tend to think of terrain as specific to rural features such as hills, valleys, mountains, rivers and so forth, it more accurately describes the "lay of the land." Thus it is equally applicable to urban environments where most of the critical features are more likely to be man-made. As a matter of fact, the effect of terrain on tactical operations in urban areas is every bit as significant as that found in rural environments. Actually, most rural landscapes are usually easier to traverse. For example, a 50-foot cliff in a rural environment may pose substantial difficulties, but a two-story wall in an urban area can be a "showstopper."

An example of the influences of urban terrain occurred while I was assigned as a team leader with one of our department's SWAT teams and a riot erupted in the Men's Central Jail in downtown Los Angeles. This jail is one of the largest jails in the free world and can house as many as 9,000 inmates.[1] In addition to the usual housing areas, there are recreational and visiting areas, stores, theaters, and even chapels and schools. The dining rooms can feed thousands of inmates at a single meal. Hallways are hundreds of yards long and are as busy as any city sidewalk at lunch hour. Virtually every accommodation of a small city exists within the confines of this custodial facility.

The riot, started by the "Crip"[2] street gang, lasted for three and a half hours before being quelled by a composite force of jail deputies and members of the SWAT team. During the subsequent debriefings, many deputies expressed the opinion that the rioters had almost succeeded in taking over a portion of the facility and that the outcome had been in doubt until the very end. Following this shocking admission, my team was assigned a research project to determine what could be done to improve our chances for success in future confrontations.

We began our research by noting that this immense building had many interior features that would impact our operations, so we began by conducting a terrain analysis. Key terrain features were identified; avenues of approach and escape were mapped out, and we ascertained potential barriers, choke points and observation posts. Our assessment revealed that terrain inside large buildings influenced the movement of

---

1. Since that time, an adjoining jail has added 1.2 million square feet and room for an additional 4,200 inmates.
2. This street gang is one of the largest and most violent in the United States. It is unknown exactly where the name "Crip" originated, but for most of the deputies and police officers who work the areas they frequent, it stands for "Cowards Run In Packs."

persons even more than the features on the outside, and tactics were developed to exploit this new understanding.

It wasn't long until our theory was put to the test when another riot erupted. This time the "Bloods"[3] seized a housing area and manufactured weapons from broken broom and mop handles, floor drains and cleaning solutions. They tied T-shirts around their faces to prevent identification. They pulled mattresses from their bunks and used them to construct barricades. They tied cell doors open or closed with strips from towels and blankets. There was serious potential for a real bloodbath. The rioters formed their ranks almost exactly as the Crips had done in the last riot. It was obvious that they expected us to confront them as we had the Crips.

After efforts to negotiate failed, a tactical intervention was called for. This time, however, one team seized a cell row above the rioters and another used a narrow aisle to channel the rioters into a narrow front—so narrow in fact that they were prevented from fighting in groups larger than four or five at any given time. The team on the high ground could determine the leaders and vulnerable areas of the rioters' formations, and both teams exploited weaknesses and opportunities as soon as they were discovered. Because of the lessons learned during the previous disturbance, this riot lasted only 12 minutes after intervention!

Conducting a Terrain Analysis

The methodical study of terrain and its effects on tactical operations has been practiced since at least 500 B.C.E., when a Chinese military strategist by the name of Sun Tzu first described it in a treatise called *The Art of War*.[4] Because some types of terrain may hinder or help the movement of persons across it, a prediction of those movements is possible. In operations attempting to resolve problems resulting from

3. Another street gang, distinguished from the Crips only by the color of their clothing.
4. "Ground equally advantageous for the enemy or me to occupy is key ground." Sun Tzu, *The Art Of War*, trans. Samuel B. Griffith (New York: Oxford University Press, 1982), p. 130.

natural disasters, such as fires or floods, terrain also plays a critical role. For example, fires burn better uphill while floods are entirely terrain-dependent. It becomes clear that an understanding of terrain is critical to the success of any tactical operation.

One of the best ways of determining the impact terrain will have on an operation is by conducting a **terrain analysis**. A terrain analysis is the process by which critical terrain features are identified and evaluated for their impact on a tactical operation. A commander who understands the influence of terrain and appropriately exploits it gains a substantial advantage over one who does not.

Conducting a terrain analysis is not a complicated procedure. The most common method involves a five-step process identified by the acronym **KOCOA**.[5] This stands for:

- **K**ey Terrain Features
- **O**bservation and Fields of Fire
- **C**over and Concealment
- **O**bstacles
- **A**venues of Approach and Escape

Key terrain is any locality, area or feature, the control of which offers a marked advantage to whoever controls it (either you or the suspect). Examples of key terrain often include high ground or tall buildings but can also include doorways that prevent a suspect from escape, or culverts and ditches that allow you a protected or unobserved approach. The point is that *any* terrain can be key terrain if it offers a marked advantage to the side that controls it.

In some cases, key terrain may dominate the scene to such an extent

---

5. KOCOA is the military acronym and the most commonly used. Some law enforcement texts, however, use "COCOA," which substitutes the term "Critical Terrain Features" for "Key Terrain Features."

that accomplishment of the overall objective hinges on control of the feature. No one will dispute the significance of the tower at the University of Texas when Charles Whitman began firing from it or a similar tower erected by the Branch Davidians near Waco, Texas. Terrain such as this is called **decisive terrain** or sometimes **commanding terrain**, and identifies any terrain feature that offers a decisive advantage. In order to ensure success, tactical operations must be designed to ensure early control of this type of terrain.

An important note is that you need not physically seize or occupy this terrain to control it. In many instances, it may not even be possible to occupy it. An example of this would be a suspect barricaded in a two-story house. If the second story is determined to be key terrain it may be possible to insert chemical agents to deprive the suspect of uninhibited access. If the suspect occupies high ground, it may be possible to deploy smoke or wait for darkness to deprive him of his ability to observe. Identifying key terrain is not enough. Key terrain is valuable *only* if it is properly exploited!

Once we understand the impact that key terrain has on our operation we need to know how to recognize it. The four other factors in terrain analysis assist in identifying types of terrain that are known to influence tactical operations, especially those features that may be critical to success.

Observation and fields of fire are closely related and are considered together. **Observation** is the surveillance that can be exercised either visually or through the use of optic or electronic devices.[6] It is important to remember that suspects have access to the same equipment as anyone else. Spotting scopes, telescopes, binoculars, night scopes and even seismic intrusion devices have been seized during arrest and search warrants.

---

6. *Ground Combat Operations*, OH 6-1, published by Commanding General, Marine Corps Combat Development Command, Quantico Virginia, 22134-5001, ¶2804, p. 221.`

A case in point occurred in Escondido, California, when a suspect was arrested for violating the state's dangerous weapons control laws. The suspect was a habitual methamphetamine user and diagnosed schizophrenic who had stopped taking his prescribed medication. Exacerbating the problem still further, he was an avid "survivalist" who was well read on the subject and was experiencing marital problems. He had a history of violence and had told neighbors that his problems were "driving him crazy."

During the investigation, officers discovered a number of rifles as well as extra magazines, ammunition and a gas mask. An alert patrol sergeant also noticed a 60-power spotting scope in an upstairs bedroom oriented at a junior high school across the street. He later related that when he looked through the scope he could even read the brand names of the children's bicycles. The significance of this did not escape the officers. The suspect was arrested and the weapons and spotting scope confiscated as evidence.

After being released on his own recognizance a few days later, the suspect bought another high-power assault rifle, returned to his apartment and fired it through the wall into an adjacent apartment. Responding officers were unable to negotiate with him and a SWAT team was called to the scene. The subsequent operation required the resources of three police departments and resulted in one police officer killed and two wounded. Throughout the operation, the suspect used the upper windows in his apartment for observation and commanded the entire vicinity by virtue of this terrain feature alone. Attempts to employ tear gas proved futile and an attempt was made to breach the apartment walls with explosives, eventually catching the building on fire and forcing the suspect into the open where he engaged officers in a fire fight, wounding another officer before he was eventually killed. During the subsequent investigation and debriefings, numerous police officers commented on how effective the lone suspect had been in preventing an approach, much less an entry.

Closely related to observation is a **field of fire**. A field of fire is defined as the area that a weapon can cover effectively from a given position. This means that it is the characteristics of the weapon and how it is deployed that define a field of fire. For instance, a sniper armed with a scoped .308 caliber rifle deployed on top of a tall building would command a considerably larger area than his spotter deployed in the same position but armed with a shotgun. The differences in the ranges of the weapons affect their respective fields of fire.

Likewise, the terrain also has an effect. Consider two identically armed snipers. One is deployed on the top of the tall building and the other is deployed looking out a window from inside. The field of fire for the sniper on top of the building is, again, considerably larger than the one inside the building, who is limited to the fan- or cone-shaped area he can see to his front.

The term "field of fire" is often confused with another similar but distinct term called a "**sector of fire**." As stated, a field of fire is that area that a weapon can cover effectively from a given position. A sector of fire, however, is an assignment that defines the limits within which a weapon is allowed to be fired. Sectors of fire keep us from shooting innocent bystanders or even each other! As Murphy says, "Friendly fire—isn't."[7] Because they are assignments, they can take any shape and may be three-dimensional. A rifleman positioned inside a skyscraper might well be given vertical as well as lateral limits.

To paraphrase, a field of fire depends upon the weapon and how it is deployed; a sector of fire is an assignment. Consequently, a sector of fire is always smaller than a field of fire. A field of fire is a factor to be considered during a terrain analysis; a sector of fire is a factor to be considered during planning.

Cover and concealment is the third step in conducting a terrain

---

7.   David Evans, "Murphy's Laws of Combat," *Amphibious Warfare Review*, Spring 1989, p. 52.

analysis. Like observation and fields of fire, cover and concealment are so closely related that they are examined together. **Cover** is anything that provides protection against fires and the effects from fires. Effects from fires would include anything that can hurt you as a result of being shot at. For example, of what advantage is it to hide behind a pressurized propane tank? Granted, the tank will likely stop the bullet, but that won't do you much good if you're killed in the ensuing explosion. Cover can be a natural or man-made terrain feature. The only requirement is that you be protected from whatever the suspect is using to shoot at you. What may be cover for one weapon may not suffice for another.

Concealment prevents observation. Thus it is an antithesis to the second step in a terrain analysis. Concealment may prevent a suspect from observing officers' movements but will not prevent injury if he fires at them. Concealment may be provided by woods, underbrush, tall grass, fences, buildings or any other feature that denies observation. Concealment may also be provided by darkness and weather conditions such as fog, snow or rain, or even artificially created by using smoke or dazzling lights directed at a suspect's position.

Because some types of concealment are temporary—darkness, for instance—it is important to understand that an operation lasting into the night or from night into day will require two different deployment plans. What may provide concealment in one light condition may allow the suspect to observe in another.

A good illustration of concealment occurred after a suspect robbed a jewelry store in Beverly Hills, California. As the suspect attempted to escape he found he was surrounded by the Beverly Hills Police Department, who established a perimeter and called a Los Angeles Sheriff's Department special weapons team. When it became obvious that the operation would continue into the night, a city maintenance worker was escorted into the perimeter and disconnected some of the streetlights. As it grew darker the suspect could detect no change. Streetlights turned on and the crime scene became illuminated. From a more distant perspective, however, *only* the crime scene was illuminated. There was a ring of darkness at the perimeter and the tactical team members remained concealed.

By recognizing the influence that cover and concealment play in tactical deployments, a commander can remain proactive and have better control. Although shooting out lights may be a viable option, it is often necessary only because of incomplete planning. This may cause an adverse effect if the suspect determines that the shots are a hostile act. As technology advances, true concealment will more realistically mean the adversary's inability to detect your presence or accurately identify your location. Advances in stealth technologies and camouflage, as well as sophisticated detection technologies, will change the way we view concealment now and in the future.

An **obstacle** is any object or terrain feature that impedes or diverts movement in an area of operation. Obstacles can be natural features like canyons, swamps and cliffs, or man-made features like walls, fences or ditches. Where vehicles are concerned, obstacles might also be closed gates, cul-de-sacs or mucky roads. Thus what may be only an inconvenience for pedestrians could be an obstacle for vehicles.

Some obstacles are so formidable that they prevent movement. Obstacles such as these are referred to as barriers. Like any other terrain feature, obstacles serve neither side unless exploited. A good tactical commander should exploit obstacles to the maximum extent possible. Obstacles may prevent a suspect from escaping or allow a perimeter to be contained with fewer personnel. Suspects often create obstacles or reinforce existing ones to prevent capture or buy time to destroy evidence.

Police usually defeat obstacles by one of two methods, bypassing or breaching. It is usually better to bypass an obstacle. Bypassing saves time, labor and risk to personnel. When it is not possible to bypass an obstacle it must be breached by opening or destroying it.

Determining **avenues of approach and escape** is the last step in a ter-

Figure 2.1 Obstacles and Barriers: Some obstacles, like the storm drain at left, are so formidable that they constitute a barrier. Others, like the gate in the photo at the right, prevent passage by one mode of movement, such as vehicles, but allow pedestrian traffic.

rain analysis. An avenue is any route by which a force can reach a tactical objective. In the case of a suspect, this might mean escape. In the case of a tactical team or team member, it might mean being able to reach a suspect's location, a vantage point or place of cover. Avenues must be broad enough to permit necessary maneuvering and bypassing of any obstacles. Too narrow an avenue and a tactical team may become constricted and canalized. This makes mutually supporting actions difficult and inhibits team members' ability to take advantage of available cover and concealment. One of the best tools for determining avenues of approach and escape is a helicopter. Terrain features that are often obscured from the ground by vegetation and adjacent buildings are easily identified from the air.

An avenue of approach or escape can be a key terrain feature if it provides a marked advantage. One example occurred when my team was assigned to serve a search warrant on a heroin dealer who was armed with a fully-automatic assault rifle. He had fortified his house with narco bars,[8] hardened his perimeter fence with barbed wire and

---

8. More commonly known as "burglar bars," these are simply steel bars affixed to doors and windows to prevent entry. They are often referred to as "narco bars" because of the proclivity of drug dealers to fortify their houses and places of business.

cut holes in his walls for shooting ports. He parked cars in his yard, which not only hindered our ability to pull the bars off but also obscured our view of any other possible entry points. In conducting the terrain analysis, an aerial photograph revealed a side door that opened to a rear yard. Access to the rear yard could be achieved from a block away, completely bypassing the suspect's fortifications. The suspect was taken completely by surprise and was unable to arm himself, despite the fact that he was sleeping with his rifle.

Coup d'Oeil Concept

While gaining an appreciation for how terrain will influence a tactical operation is critical, it is only valuable if exploited. The success of a tactical operation often hinges on a commander's ability to quickly determine and exploit a weakness in a suspect's position. The ability to identify weaknesses in a suspect's position can be described and explained with a concept called "**coup d'oeil**" (pronounced koo dwee). Coup d'oeil is a French expression that, loosely translated, means the "strike of the eye" or the "vision behind the eye." The closest English concept would be that of intuition. Intuition is defined as "perceptive insight" or "the power to discern the true nature of a situation." It explains a commander's ability to "see" what the terrain looks like on the other side of a hill or the floor plan of the inside of a building coupled with an understanding of the impact they have on the operation.

A suspect's weakness can be related to a position, as when he finds himself vulnerable from an avenue of approach or an inability to observe. Or it can be related to timing, as when he is presented with more possibilities than he can effectively cope with. Thus a commander benefits from an ability not only to see the potential of a maneuver but also to envision the future. When time is the primary factor, this might involve envisioning situations that cause a suspect to react in some predictable manner that can then be exploited. When position is the primary

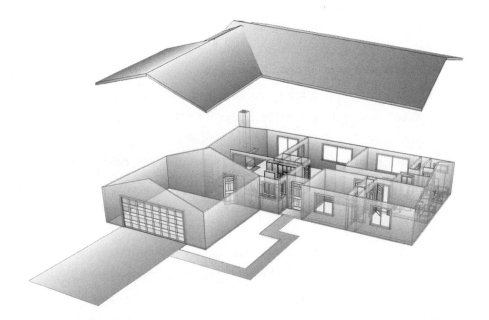

Figure 2.2 Coup d'Oeil Concept: With tactical diagramming, the coup d'oeil concept explains a commander's apparent ability to "see" what the floor plan of a building might look like coupled with the influence it will have on an operation. Tactical diagramming provides a means to enhance this ability.

factor, the commander will anticipate a suspect's ability or inability to watch more than one avenue of approach or simultaneously protect an avenue of approach and control some other key terrain.

While commanders who possess visual intuition might be considered gifted, it is more likely that their abilities have been developed. The coup d'oeil concept involves judgment, and judgment can be enhanced through education, training and experience.

Prominent Terrain and Micro-Terrain

Because most law enforcement tactical operations occur on urban terrain, tactical diagramming is simply an extension of a terrain analysis. An ability to predict a floor plan allows more precise planning and can provide vital information by revealing key terrain inside a building, regardless of its size. A reliable diagram will assist in predicting where a suspect is likely to be, where he might go and even what he might do when placed in the context of other tactical intelligence. To effectively and efficiently employ tactical diagrams, however, two additional terrain features need to be understood.

Prominent terrain is any terrain feature that can be easily identified and is displayed on a map or diagram. Prominent terrain often includes features such as hills, road intersections, rivers and bridges, as well as cultural landmarks such as churches, schools or courthouses. Prominent terrain is most often used to orient a person as to direction and distance. When diagrams are employed, prominent terrain can be designated. This means that some terrain that is too small to be displayed on a map but so distinctive that it can't be mistaken may provide the equivalent of a signpost. Examples may include brightly colored roofs, swimming pools or uniquely shaped trees. Such features are prominent *only* when identified on the diagram and used as a vector.

Micro-terrain is simply terrain that will have an impact on your operation but is too small or insignificant to be depicted on a map. Examples of micro-terrain may include sheds, rocks, fences, plants or ditches. It is micro-terrain that makes field sketches and diagrams necessary. In tactical diagramming, it might include large features such as the shape and orientation of a house to the street or more diminutive features such as where a door is located and which way it swings. Thus tactical diagramming may include prominent terrain but always includes micro-terrain.

CHAPTER 3

The Urban Landscape

Characteristics of the Urban Landscape

While there is no denying that many law enforcement tactical operations occur in rural regions, most occur in urban areas. This is probably because about 80 percent of Americans live in urban areas and urban areas have a higher crime rate. When considering the uses of tactical diagramming it is even more relevant, because by definition there are more buildings in cities. Consequently, an understanding of urban terrain is of great aid in understanding and applying techniques for tactical diagramming. While there are any number of differences between rural and urban terrain, seven are especially critical for tactical planning.

Figure 3.1 Urban Landscape: The urban landscape is more diverse than most people realize and may appear dramatically different from rural landscapes; nevertheless, the fundamentals of terrain analysis remain the same. These photographs were taken a few feet from each other on opposite sides of the same hill.

First, urban terrain provides a **definite defensive advantage**. Even the least experienced adversary quickly learns to exploit the easily fortified positions that offer cover and concealment. First responders, such as law enforcement, fire fighters and other emergency services, must maneuver over terrain that makes them vulnerable to bricks, rocks, bottles and other missiles thrown from upper stories and behind buildings, or even gunfire from rooftops, windows and doorways. Furthermore, roads, streets and alleys constrict the avenues of approach and escape. This makes outside movement highly predictable and relatively easily detected.

Second, urban terrain has a **three-dimensional quality** that is lacking in rural environments. Traversing rural terrain must be done on the same horizontal plane; that is, except in the extremely rare instances of caves, tunnels and mines, personnel and vehicles are limited to the two dimensions of length and width. In contrast, buildings in the urban environment are the hollow counterparts of hills and peaks in rural terrain. Fleeing suspects can easily move up and down multiple-story buildings, through basements, sewers, ducts, crawl spaces and attics. To a greater or lesser extent, every building provides concealment, if not cover, that suspects can easily exploit to great tactical advantage, and each presents a somewhat unique and formidable tactical challenge. Consequently, when analyzing urban terrain a vertical dimension must also be considered because of the abundance of vantage points and avenues of approach and escape above and below the horizontal plane.

Third, adversaries are typically **engaged at extremely close ranges**, usually less than 20 feet and often half that distance.[1] Gunfights regularly occur inside buildings where even a large room is substantially less than 20 feet. Targets appear fleeting and along restricted lines of

---

1. Approximately 90 percent of all officer-involved shootings occur at less than 20 feet and about 75 percent occur at about 10 feet. Rick Baratta, "Firearms Training," *Law and Order Magazine*, March 1999, p. 65.

Figure 3.2 Compartmented Terrain: Besides being three-dimensional, urban terrain is "chopped" into well-defined pathways by streets, alleys, drainage ditches and buildings, as well as hallways, doorways and stairways inside buildings. This characteristic affects both movement and tactics.

sight because urban terrain is far more compartmented and channelized than rural terrain. The presence of buildings, streets, alleys and drainage ditches "chops" the terrain into well-defined pathways that are nearly impossible to avoid. Inside buildings are doorways, hallways and stairways that force personnel into constricted "choke points" and make them vulnerable to detection and attack. Moving vehicles and personnel are nearly always limited to those passageways and avenues specifically intended for them. Even hastily constructed obstacles can pose formidable challenges. A criminal sniper in the urban environment is more likely to be armed with a handgun at ground level or in a vehicle and to take shots of opportunity than to use a long rifle from an established position.

Fourth, **communications over urban terrain are frequently unreliable and sporadic**. Coupled with spontaneous and brief encounters at close ranges, the necessity for decentralized control becomes apparent. Small teams are required to operate almost independently, yet rely upon adjacent teams for reinforcements and higher headquarters for logistical support and sustainment. Consequently, centralized planning is critical and deployed units must be more autonomous and capable of operating without detailed instructions.

Fifth, the urban environment, almost by definition, is accompanied by the **presence of a civilian population**. While most would not consider the presence of people as a terrain feature, I mention it here because you ignore it at your own peril. Only a neophyte will fail to understand that there is virtually no place in the city where there is an assurance that movement will not be observed. Consequently, time of day can be as important as the choice of route. Moreover, a trained observer can use the activities and actions of the populace as indicators for impending trouble. The sudden disappearance of bystanders or shoppers can be as conspicuous and precipitous as the sudden flight of birds or the hasty retreat of a deer with its tail up in the rural environment. Thus a fourth dimension, time, becomes critical to the terrain analysis.

Sixth, unlike the rural environment, which has few reflective surfaces and no direct lighting, the urban environment has both. This results in **uneven ambient light** and harsh shadows adjacent to glaring lights. This characteristic makes it nearly impossible to gain night vision and offers hiding places in "plain view." This is because the pupil of the human eye will constrict in about half a second when exposed to bright light but takes about two minutes to dilate in low light. Additionally, night vision is largely gained through a fluid in the eye called rhodopsin.[2] In low light, this fluid is dark-colored and easily gathers light energy in much the same way that dark clothing absorbs heat. When exposed to bright light, however, it quickly "bleaches out" and can take

---

2. Sometimes called "visual purple."

as long as 30 minutes to return to its darker color and light-gathering efficiency. Persons obscured in shadow may be completely invisible but have an unobstructed view of the surroundings.

This characteristic also has a vertical aspect. Generally, the brightest lights and harshest shadows are at ground level up to about the second floor of buildings. This is the area that has direct lighting from street lights, illuminated signs and windows, with many highly reflective surfaces such as sidewalks, pavement, buildings and glass. It is also in this area that seemingly opaque areas of darkness exist because they are shielded from lights by awnings, walls, fences, trees and shrubs. The second area is slightly darker and more even in lighting and begins from above the height of street lights to the tops of the adjacent buildings. It shares many of the same features as the lower zone but with less direct lighting and fewer obstacles to create dark shadows. The last zone is on the rooftops. This zone shares many of the same lighting attributes as does the rural environment, such as moonlight and starlight, and consequently night vision and the use of night vision goggles offer substantial advantages.

Last, buildings in the city are more than terrain features **because buildings have value**. This means that in addition to tactical significance, a building may also have cultural, historical, religious or political importance. Churches, synagogues, museums, city halls and so forth are only a few examples. Thus there are often considerations besides tactics that might limit movement, prohibit damage, or even entry.

Navigating Urban Terrain

When it comes to navigating urban terrain in the United States, most people immediately think of street addresses. While this method is practical for most purposes, it falls short in tactical operations. Search and arrest warrants, for example, require both a street address and a detailed description. The description is intended to be so specific that a person looking for a particular house or building will be able to identify it even if no street numbers are present. Likewise, street addresses are insufficient for coordinating components of a tactical operation because they identify only a piece of property. Tactical teams that must move within the property need a more precise means of orienting and navigating. It becomes clear that an understanding of how urban terrain is divided, identified and used for orientation is useful for tactical coordination and planning.

Property Identification

The American street address system is the end result of a complicated evolution of previous methods for identifying property. The predominant older system, called "metes and bounds,"[3] is a primitive way of identifying property that used terrain features as index points and lines. It was easy to employ, requiring no skills in surveying, because it used features like rivers and roads as property lines, and trees and rocks as reference marks.[4] Problems arose, however, when over time a riverbed changed, a tree was destroyed by fire or a road was rerouted. You can imagine the problems this created as the country matured and disputes arose. In fact, there are disputes based upon this system that last to this day.[5]

To avoid future problems, a new system called the Public Land Survey System[6] was implemented when settlers began moving west after the Revolutionary War. Designed by Thomas Jefferson, this system subdivides lands into "tracts" of about 24 miles square and then

---

3. "Metes and bounds" may be more commonly understood as "bearings and distances" from specific natural or man-made monuments.
4. These reference marks are called "monuments" and can be any durable and fixed mark, feature or object that can be easily identified. A monument can be natural or man-made.
5. Survey systems for all the thirteen original states, plus Texas, Tennessee, Kentucky, West Virginia, Vermont, Maine and Hawaii are based on this system, and Louisiana's original surveys are based on the French "long lot" system. This tremendously complicates property identification and ownership.
6. This system is also known as the Land Ordinance of 1785, the Government Survey System, the Rectangular Survey System, or the Township and Range System.

into "townships" of approximately 6 miles square. Each township is further divided into "sections" that are one mile square and equal to about 640 acres. In urban areas, sections are always further subdivided into half-sections, quarter-sections and even smaller lots. In fact, the modern term "subdivision," identifying a tract of houses, is taken from this surveying method. The measurements for these parcels are taken from surveyed range lines, (sometimes called meridians), which are true north-south lines,[7] and base lines, which are true east-west lines. The influence of this system can be easily seen from an airplane by observing the grid-like system of roads and streets and neat rectangles of fields and city lots. Many cities also have roads and streets named "Baseline," "Range," or "Meridian."

Street Addresses

When the population of an area became sufficiently dense to require some more precise method of quickly identifying a piece of property, especially for mail delivery, house numbering schemes were developed. These vary from jurisdiction to jurisdiction, but some common conventions have evolved. For example, the numbering system almost always begins at the center of a locale and moves outward. In urban areas these are often the historical centers of the towns and are identified by names such as Main Street or Central Avenue. In rural areas, it is frequently Range Road, Baseline Road, Line Road and the like. Rural areas often use five numbers to identify a house, and cities usually use three or four numbers. This is also useful because a change in jurisdiction is frequently conspicuous when the house numbers "jump" from one scheme to another.

---

7. There are actually three navigational north poles. "Magnetic north" is dictated by the earth's magnetic field and is where compasses point. It is currently located in northern Canada. "Grid north" is used to allow the three-dimensional globe to be depicted on two-dimensional maps. "True north" is the geographic North Pole where all longitudinal lines converge to a single point.

Since many large metropolitan areas evolved after the land was surveyed and sold, the subdivisions followed the same scheme. This also contributed to conventions when city blocks were built to provide access to small lots because square miles (sections) were divided into eight city blocks and sometimes into sixteen. Each mile normally has 100 separate addresses, almost always alternating with odd numbers on one side of the street or road and even numbers on the other. Thus, in a city using numbered streets like 87th Street, 88th Avenue and the like, the named streets are often, but not always, 1 mile or 1/8 mile apart. The custom of alternating odd/even numbers on opposite sides of the streets led to another convention of placing the odd numbers on the north sides of east-west streets and the west sides of north-south streets and the even numbers on the opposite sides. When more precision is required, the property numbers are usually designated in fractions or letters. Thus a large office or apartment building may have a single numerical address with scores of offices or apartments and suites individually designated by letters or another set of numbers.

Another common practice that is of aid in navigating urban terrain is the custom of each jurisdiction adopting a different style and color for its street signs. Even if a numbering scheme continues through more than one jurisdiction, the street signs will often change color, style or design. In many areas, questions arising such as "who has the authority and responsibility for . . ." can be resolved by simply looking at the nearest street sign.

Zip Codes

While zip codes may seem superfluous for tactical operations, they are frequently used as an index to all kinds of information that may have tactical importance. Furthermore, the zip code itself is a scheme that can be used to identify geographical locations anywhere in the country.

"Zip" actually stands for "Zoning Improvement Program," and

Figure 3.3 Street Signs: While the urban landscape is full of navigation aids, some can be subtle to all but the trained observer. Here the styles of the street signs indicate different jurisdictions for the same street.

codes were introduced in 1963 to simplify mail distribution. Zip codes were originally five-digit numbers designed to be placed after street addresses to assist postal workers in expediting mail delivery. The first number designates one of ten geographical areas in the United States and its possessions, beginning with "0" in the northeast and ending with "9" in the west. The next four digits subdivided the major geographical areas. Consequently, the first three digits of a zip code can be used to identify a major regional or metropolitan area and the last two to identify an associated or branch post office. In October 1983, the system was further refined with an additional four digits that designate an individual delivery route.

As the years have passed, zip codes have been used for many things besides mail delivery. For example, the proximity of various locations to one another can be quickly estimated by comparing zip codes. This has led to their use as indices for car pool databases, mapping programs and market analysis. Because they precisely identify geographical regions, zip codes are often used to augment census tracts and demographical analysis studies. Insurance companies use them for estimating risks, especially for automobile and house insurance. Real estate agents use them for estimating local property values. Zip codes are also used to index databases for telephone numbers and time zones, latitude/longitude, congressional and school districts, real estate and financial information, and so many other categories that it is impossible to do more than point out their significance. Likewise, their potential for providing information of tactical value should not be overlooked.

Tactical Numbering System

As modern law enforcement tactical teams began evolving in the mid to late 1960s, a number of procedural problems arose in orienting team members in urban settings because of the difficulty in precisely identifying specific buildings. Cardinal directions do not work very well in the city because they tend to be imprecise when looking for a small and specific location. Moreover, magnetic compasses are heavily influenced by localized magnetic fields such as vehicles and metallic building infrastructures. Compounding the problem still further is that prominent terrain features are frequently obscured by nearby trees and buildings. And, because street addresses are seldom displayed from alleys or the backs of property and buildings, and most houses, especially tract houses, lack easily distinguishable markings, orientation became exceedingly difficult. The solution was to develop a "work around" navigational system to augment those already in existence to facilitate coordination and control of the many moving components of tactical teams.

As the years have passed, a number of navigational systems have been developed by tactical teams, but regardless of which system is employed, there are some common criteria. First, the system must be easily and readily understood. The idea is to aid understanding, not to arbitrarily superimpose an additional navigational system. Second, it should augment, not replace existing systems. The idea here is not to reinvent the wheel. City maps and street addresses work just fine to locate a piece of property. Tactical navigational systems pick up where addresses leave off by providing orientation for moving within the property boundaries and micro-terrain. Last, it should have universal application, or at least the broadest application possible, to avoid encountering situations that would require the system to be appended still further and create more confusion.

One of the best I've seen uses a versatile, alpha-numeric method that can be easily and clearly transmitted on radios and annotated on maps and diagrams while providing information on the observer's perspective. It works like this: The first number always represents a side of the first story beginning with the front and continuing around the building clockwise. The front is *always* designated, but the side facing the street is usually the one chosen, and is designated the 1-side.[8] Moving clockwise, the second side of the building is designated the 2-side, and so forth. Corners can be designated as the 2-3 corner, the 1-4 corner etc. This system works even though buildings are seldom perfectly rectangular because small alcoves and walls perpendicular to the primary side are considered as part of that side. This system will work "as is" for almost all buildings up to about three or four floors.

When multiple-story buildings are encountered, letters are used to designate a specific story. This is only necessary when there are more than three stories, since "plain text" is preferred for clarity and ease of understanding. Letters are used only to substitute for an elaborate description. For example, a sniper firing from a window of the sixth

---

8. To avoid confusion, the Team Leader or the Scout of the team will designate which side will be used for the 1-side. This method becomes especially critical when the main entrance does not face the street.

Figure 3.4 Numbering System: One of the most versatile and easy-to-use navigation aids for buildings employs a number system. It works by identifying the main entrance and labeling it as the 1 side and then continuing clockwise around the building. Corners are designated by a combination of numbers, such as the 3-4 corner. Plain English is used when more precision is required.

floor at the back of a large apartment building can be identified as 3F3, meaning that he is at the back of the building, firing from the sixth floor and the third window from the extreme left corner of that side. While there are other systems that may provide more precision, they usually do so at the cost of clarity and understanding. Consequently, plain English is preferred, even though it takes more time and requires more effort.

This system can also be used for orientation, coordinating movements and immediate deployments. To use it for orientation, any team member can precisely identify a portion of the building or terrain feature with a "known point." For example, a team member on containment who sees a suspect hiding near a tree at the rear of the building may radio, "Suspect is near the tree at the 2-3 corner of the building next to a lawn shed." The "2-3 corner" tells everyone the approximate location, which is then made more precise with any additional information in plain text. It can also be used from outside to inside and vice versa, as in a containment team member advising, "There is a window on the second story of the 4-side that overlooks the yard." An entry team inside the building might then seek out that window to provide coordinating information for outside personnel. To use the system for movement, a team member may describe which side of a building presents the best avenue of approach or where a vantage point may provide observation. For example, instructions can be transmitted to the effect of "From the large palm tree on the 1-4 corner of the house, move along the 4-side to the 3-4 corner."

Immediate deployments present special problems for tactical teams because the need for a response outweighs the need for precision. These are often the result of life-or-death situations and present extraordinary difficulties for coordination and movement. To use this system for an immediate deployment, a building is mentally divided in half diagonally from the 1-2 corner to the 3-4 corner. Thus the 1-side and the 4-side form one half and the 2-side and the 3-side form the other half. These sections are commonly called the Front Five and the Rear Five.

A team confronted with a situation requiring immediate deployment simply responds to the scene with one component taking positions along the "Front Five" and another component taking positions along the "Rear Five." As they find positions of tactical advantage, they call them in to the Command Post, who plots them on a rough sketch. The call-signs are generally taken from the side of the building where a team member is deployed. For example, a sniper deployed at the rear of the building would be designated Sniper #3 and one along the 4-side would be Sniper #4. In the same manner, other members performing functions such as spotter,[9] gas grenadiers and so forth take their positions and call signs from the side of the building where they are deployed.

Once the team is in place, everyone listening can identify not only the assignment but the perspective they have on the building. A sniper reporting movement might say, "Sniper #3 is advising a curtain is moving at the second-floor window on the 3 side nearest the 3-4 corner." Using this system, team members who have never seen that side of the building can form a reliable mental image[10] of the observer's perspective, where the movement is, the location of adjacent team members and who might become involved in a potential course of action.

---

9. A spotter is an observer usually, but not always, deployed with a sniper.
10. This mental image is critical for tactical planning and is more fully explained in the "coup d'oeil concept." See Terrain Analysis, Chapter 2.

CHAPTER 4

Housing Trends

Our homes reveal more about our behavior, personality, mannerisms and habits than any other material facet of our lives. Regardless of how well we succeed in presenting a public persona, our homes reveal an inner character that is impossible to conceal. A five-minute exploration of a home divulges the owners' interests and hobbies, their pets, their tastes in clothing, decorating, music and food, even how many children they have and their ages, sexes and interests. When we visit other people's homes we interpret subtle clues to form highly accurate conclusions regarding aspects of their lives that they may never have intended to reveal. It is why adoption agencies almost always require a home visit as part of the application process.

From a law enforcement tactical standpoint, residences are where the vast majority of our confrontations occur. They are the scenes of countless domestic disputes, drug transactions, search warrants, child abuse calls, loud parties, barricaded suspects and hostage incidents. Accordingly, an ability to determine floor plans from outside the building can provide substantial tactical advantages.

There are any number of influences that affect the design, style and size of our homes, and none occur in isolation from the others. While it may seem overly simplistic to describe them as if they each occur without being influenced by the others, it facilitates clarity and

understanding if I break them into broad categories. A solid understanding of these influences will be especially important in tactical
diagramming when more precise clues are missing or ambiguous and
assumptions must be made.

Sociological Influences

Homes reflect sociological influences and values just as much as styles
of dress or choices of vehicle. For determining floor plans, however,
they have one major advantage: they are more enduring. In fact, about
three quarters of all existing houses have been built since 1940[1] and
almost 43 percent have been built since 1970. This means that about
70 percent of the 110 million housing units in the United States today
will still be around two decades from now. The 100-year-old house
is the exception, not the rule.[2] This simplifies the task of determining
floor plans because it tends to attenuate older influences. Anyone who
has ever remodeled a house will attest to the great expense and effort it
takes, and the task is greatly compounded if walls need to be moved. As
a result, even houses that have been remodeled, refurbished or renovated[3] often keep the same or very similar floor plans. Nevertheless, there
are some substantial differences between older and newer houses, and
an understanding of the sociological influences provides a conceptual
framework of understanding.

One of the greatest sociological impacts on the size and design of

---

1. Witold Rybczynski, *Looking Around: A Journey Through Architecture* (New York: Viking, 1993),
   p. 74.
2. Most of the older houses are in the Northeast, followed by the Midwest, with most of the newer
   construction in the South and West portions of the country.
3. While most people believe that "remodel," "refurbish" and "renovate" are synonyms, there are
   subtle differences, and the building trades understand them to be distinct and different. Remodeling
   involves reconstructing to enhance appearance, provide additional room and/or functions or adapt
   to a social change. Renovating involves modernizing a structure to update it and/or exploit new
   technologies and appliances. Refurbishing or restoring requires reconditioning or rejuvenating a
   structure to its original condition. Of the three, remodeling is not only the most common but also
   the most likely to affect floor plans and interior design.

Figure 4.1 Alleys: One of the first steps in diagramming a house is to estimate its age. Here, the presence of alleys and detached garages in the neighborhood indicates an older part of the city.

our homes is our idea of family. When we lived on farms, large families were needed to attend to the multitude of chores. When people flocked to the cities during the industrial age, the concept of a family changed very slowly. Families remained large and often included grandparents. Consequently, the houses looked very similar to their rural counterparts. They tended to be large and multi-story with large porches that faced toward the street. The bedrooms were upstairs and the living room was downstairs at the front (street side) of the house. Outbuildings, like sheds and garages, were at the rear of the lot facing the opposite direction, usually to a common access such as an alley.

But as time passed, families grew smaller and grandparents more often lived in their own homes. The need for large homes diminished and smaller homes became more popular. The trend was accentuated in the 1930s and 1940s with the Great Depression and World War II, when people could not afford to build large houses. After the war, returning GIs wanted the "American Dream," and small, cottage-like homes were relatively inexpensive and appealing. During this time the typical family had Dad, working at the office or factory, and Mom, staying home to take care of the two children. In fact, by 2000 the average number of occupants in a house was only 2.6 people.[4] With more affluence in recent times, the inclusion of home offices, great rooms and multiple bathrooms became popular and the trend was reversed. The average size of a home built since the 1990s is now about 2,161 square feet.[5]

Just as dramatic was the change in social climate. The city was not as safe as the country and the designs of homes began to reflect the apprehension of the occupants. The large, multi-story houses with the front porch looking out toward the street that was popular in the country underwent drastic reductions in size and changes in design. The living areas facing the street were turned around and now looked toward the rear of the property onto a large, fenced (or walled) back yard. The "back"[6] door that entered into a small porch-like area and then to the kitchen on the older homes was replaced by sliding or French doors between a family room and a patio at the rear of the newer homes. The upstairs bedrooms in the older homes were moved downstairs and to one end of a single-story structure. The large porches gradually shrank in size to only about 12 to 16 square feet. Unlike the original porches, these "entryways" were never designed for family functions but sim-

---

4. *Housing Facts, Figures & Trends, 2004* (Washington, D.C.: National Association of Home Builders, 2004), p. 33.
5. Taken from a U.S. Census Report entitled *These Old Houses*, as reported by Rice and Alison, "Old Vs. New," *Builder*, April 2004, p. 61.
6. More often located on a side of the house, especially the driveway side.

ply to channel visitors to an area where the occupants could screen them before granting entry.

As we move into the future, other sociological influences are beginning to affect the design of houses, most notably the "cottage industry." The trend toward working at home is not new. Indeed, in early American times most people worked out of their houses. As we move from the industrial age to the information age, the advent of telephones, fax machines, computers and, most importantly, the Internet, makes where a person is physically working less and less relevant. This is reflected in newer houses being equipped with fully functional home offices. Consequently, homes are becoming larger again. Home offices, a three-car attached garage, two or more bathrooms[7] and often a guest room are becoming the norm.

As a result of these sociological influences, American houses tend to be eclectic, composed of elements and influences of more than one style and period. While salespeople will talk about a "ranch style" or "Cape Cod" house as if it were the latest model of automobile, American houses are nearly never purely one style, and even if they began that way, the owners soon adapt them to their individual tastes. Thus an understanding of the local culture and homeowner's interests, likes and dislikes can have a substantial influence when a house is constructed or remodeled. This is particularly so if the owner has lived in the home for a long time.

Technological Influences

While most people wouldn't think of technology and houses together, technology has affected home design in two fundamental ways. The first is what they are made of. For example, when asked to describe the building materials for a house, most people would itemize things

---

7. Nearly 94 percent of houses constructed since 1990 have more than one bathroom (includes half-baths).

like wood, concrete, drywall, nails and glass. Not very "high tech," to be sure. But improvements in building materials and components have allowed designs that older materials and technologies couldn't support. One example is the increased off-site construction of components that can be mass-produced at factories and then transported and erected at the building site. Trusses, for example, have become more and more prevalent since they were first introduced to the American home building industry in 1952. Trusses allow larger rooms because they distribute weight more efficiently than the older post and beam type of construction. Zero-clearance fireplaces can be installed in upper stories without requiring masonry support or chimneys and have become almost standard in upstairs family and living rooms or the master bedroom. Other innovations such as drywall,[8] plywood, pre-hung doors, plastic plumbing and vinyl siding have decreased the prices overall and permitted home buyers to afford larger houses in general.

The second technological influence is what goes inside houses. I'm not talking about the kind of technology that goes into high-definition television and microwave ovens, which are only mildly interesting when it comes to tactical diagramming. For our purposes, the most relevant innovations are those that affect the floor plans. Take bathrooms, for example. While most of us would have difficulty imagining a house without an indoor bathroom, bathrooms didn't really come inside until the 1920s. Now, however, multiple bathrooms are the norm. About the same time, electricity became standard in homes, which brought electric lights and refrigerators. The modern dishwasher wasn't prevalent until the 1960s, and the trash compactor came along still later. Nevertheless, floor plans were altered because these appliances brought greater convenience, and the old "service porch" at the back door that was used for hanging coats, washing clothes and storing trash has all but disappeared.

---

8. Sometimes called "plasterboard."

Popular Appliances and Technologies for New Homes[9]	
Appliances	
• Ranges, cook tops and ovens	95%
• Dishwasher	93%
• Garbage disposer	77%
• Microwave	72%
• Refrigerator	40%
• Clothes dryer and washer	19%
• Central vacuum	10%
• Trash compactor	5%
Technologies	**Percent installed in new homes**
• Multi-line phone system	38.4%
• Security system—alerts protective service	23.3%
• Security system—sounds alarm in house	17.3%
• Whole-house audio system	7.2%
• Intercom/entrance phone	5.8%
• Built-in home theater	4.6%
• Whole-house video system	4.6%

Figure 4.2 Appliances and Technologies

Now there are walk-in pantries near the kitchen and coat closets near the front door, and the washer and dryer have been moved to the attached garage or their own "laundry room." The home office has been added to include an ISDN or a DSL line,[10] computers, printers, fax machines and the like.

---

9. *Housing Facts, Figures & Trends, 2004* (Washington, D.C.: National Association of Home Builders, 2004), pp. 6–10.
10. Both ISDN (Integrated Services Digital Network) and DSL (Digital Subscriber Line) provide high-speed Internet connections over conventional telephone lines.

Environmental Influences

Every house is a "mini-environment" in its own right because it has been specifically designed to protect us from the natural elements. We condition our inside air by heating or cooling it and sometimes by adding moisture or drying it. We pay little heed to the night because we control our interior lighting. We insulate our walls to avoid extreme outside temperatures and noise. Climatic conditions also affect home design. Houses in the East and Midwest must contend with snow loads. Those in the Southwest protect from heat. In fact, the design of buildings is probably more strongly influenced by the environment than by any other factor. Regardless of where a building is located, there are four fundamental factors with which they must all contend. These are gravity, wind, water and fire. Each of these affects a building's design, and if we are to accurately predict their floor plans, we must understand their influences.

Gravity is the ubiquitous force to which all buildings eventually succumb. Regardless of whatever else is attacking a building, be it fire, wind or water, gravity is what brings it down. It is the force that makes poor construction and building materials conspicuous when cracks appear at

Figure 4.3 Environmental Comparisons: Climatic conditions affect house design. The house on the left has steeper roofs to shed water and prevent snow buildup, and the narrow eaves allow the sun to warm the house and the walls naturally. In hotter climates, flatter roofs, like the house on the right, prevent hot attic air from radiating into the house and the large eaves shade the walls from hot sun.

the upper corners of doors and windows, when doors don't hang straight and windows won't open or close. It is also the elemental force that must be defeated to support floors, ceilings and roofs and allow the open spaces in between. And because of gravity, there are limitations to how much weight can be supported over distance. Once these are understood, the size of rooms can be predicted with some assurance.

Generally, wind is not a serious concern for residences and other small buildings, but it can have a major effect on other types of buildings by putting constraints on their size, shape, location and orientation. Even on small buildings, however, gable roofs with large eaves may tend to lift where heavy winds are prevalent, and flat roofs with parapets may create a vortex that causes a vacuum behind the parapet with the same results.

Buildings are affected by water in three different ways. The first is precipitation. Roofs must shed snow and rain and divert it for drainage. Walls, doors and windows must keep out moisture. The second is ground water, which must be kept out of and away from the footings and foundation and not allowed to seep into basements and crawl spaces. The third is the water that we keep inside the buildings for drinking, eating, cooking, washing and to flush away wastes. Of the three, the water we intentionally keep inside buildings has the most effect on floor plans, primarily because the pipes and vents are built into the walls. We'll delve into the implications of this aspect in some detail later in the book.

By far, even more than gravity, fire has had the most significant impact on the floor plans of all buildings, including residences. The early building codes were instigated because of unsafe structures, and fire is still the number one cause of death inside buildings. Laws relating to fire hazards will dictate everything from the type of building materials to the permitted use of the building. They regulate the size of rooms, number and size of doors, where they are located, and the size of the windows and how close to the floor they must be. In fact, there is not a single building under the jurisdiction of any building code in the United States that isn't required to meet some provision relating to fire safety. Consequently, many of the requirements that dictate how a building must be constructed and used can also be put to use to determine the floor plans.

Economic Influences

Almost without exception, a person's house is the single most expensive purchase they will ever make. Economic factors are usually pivotal in a person's choice of where to buy, what to build, and even what materials to use. In fact, styles of housing are viewed as a reflection of a person's financial worth.

A number of major and relatively recent economic influences have changed the way we live. One of the first was the industrial revolution that began in the United States in the mid nineteenth century and lasted well into the twentieth century. Mass production for manufacturing and industry required lots of local labor. High wages offered strong incentives and people flocked to the cities in unprecedented numbers. Initially these people lived in whatever shelter was available, often in sheds, basements, or in the factories where they worked. As they became more affluent and could afford to build houses, they patterned them after the traditional "farm house," which many still remembered with fondness, or the much smaller and less expensive "row house."

The more affluent built larger houses, often reaching 3,000 square feet or more, with large porches and two stories.[11] When garages became necessary, they were outbuildings set back from the house, usually on a side or back yard and often facing the opposite direction into an alley. These types of houses can still be seen in older portions of cities but have often been subdivided into apartments or condominiums.

The less prosperous lived in row houses modeled after architectural

---

11. More than 80 percent of homes built before 1920 in the Northeast and 63 percent in the Midwest (where most of the nation's older homes are located) included three or more stories.

styles such as the Queen Anne Cottage or the Classic Box. These houses were built identically, side by side, row upon row—hence the name. They were small, single-story, often with a bay window facing the street and narrow side yards between them. These houses often used a hip roof with a dormer but almost never had living space above the first floor.

The second major economic influence was the Great Depression, when the American dream of owning a home was a largely unattainable one. Land was becoming scarce and more expensive. Large houses were nearly impossible to afford. The population shift was continuing, however, and cities were steadily growing larger and larger. The bungalow filled the bill by providing a style that could be easily constructed at a reasonable cost, didn't require much acreage and used more modern building materials. This style uses no hallways or formal parlors and is frequently described in a realtor's brochure as "cozy." These houses have withstood the test of time and remain unchanged as they comprise the older residential districts of many large cities, especially in the West.

The post–World War II era brought a period of affluence to the housing market, again reflected by changes in styles, sizes and building materials. While the smaller houses were still popular with returning GIs attending school or beginning new jobs, by the 1950s these began to give way to more modern designs such as the ranch style. This style tends to be larger but usually has only one story, and is often built in an L-shape or U-shape configuration. Porches all but disappeared and were replaced with small entryways at the front door and patios at the rear. Personal transportation was now considered a necessity and two-car attached garages became standard.[12]

As the industrial age begins to be replaced by the information age, the design of houses has again begun to reflect economic changes. Two

---

12. Currently, more than 90 percent of new homes include a garage.

are of particular importance: the growth of cottage industries and the prevalence of telecommuting.

"Cottage industries" is a term used to broadly describe all manner of personal businesses done in the home, such as accounting, billing, bookkeeping, drafting, crafts, childcare or dressmaking. It reflects a return to personal attention and unique goods instead of mass-produced merchandise. Likewise, the invention and widespread use of microcomputers, fax machines and the Internet have encouraged people to work at home. These economic influences are reflected in housing design by the addition of home offices and large houses and will continue through the foreseeable future.

Political Influences

The fact that we pass laws to protect our homes should come as no great surprise to any American. In terms of privacy, homes are among the most protected areas of our lives and a fundamental component of our Bill of Rights.[13] Even more important for our purposes are the codes that circumscribe how buildings are constructed, because these laws provide strong clues to our ultimate goal of determining floor plans from outside architectural features.

The first building codes began to appear in the United States in the 1920s. In 1922, the International Conference of Building Officials was founded and provided a model code. This organization publishes the most popular of the model building codes, called the *Uniform Building Code*. This code is revised and republished every three years, and most communities routinely adopt the latest revisions. Two other model codes are published by the Building Officials and Code Administrators International and the Southern Building Code Congress International,

---

13. The Third Amendment of the U.S. Constitution requires the consent of the owner of a house to quarter soldiers, and the Fourth Amendment deals specifically with the people's right to be "secure in their persons, homes, papers and effects."

Figure 4.4 Zoning Influences: The various zones are easily discerned in this aerial view of a large city with clusters of commercial, manufacturing and residential buildings. Zoning laws are nearly always local ordinances and restrict everything from the use and size of the building to where it sits on a lot and even the type of siding and roofing allowed.

but the *Uniform Building Code* is the most widely adopted. Even so, for our purposes, there's not much difference between any of the building codes.

Another set of laws that affect building design are zoning ordinances. Zoning ordinances are similar to building codes except that they prescribe what kind of building can be constructed in a location rather than how it must be constructed. There are at least four major zoning categories. These are residential—where we live; industrial—where our goods and wares are produced; agricultural—where food is grown and processed; and commercial—where our merchandise is sold. Each of these categories is often divided still further, usually identified by a number. For example, residential zones may be further divided into zones for single-family dwellings (R-1, houses), multiple-family dwellings (R-2, duplexes), and high-density residences (R-3, apartments and condominiums). The same can be said for the other three categories. Zoning ordinances can also set limits on such things as the minimum lot size, height and size of buildings, how far they must be from a property line, and even their décor. Like building codes, zoning ordinances provide strong clues to how a building is used, which has a direct impact on the design and floor plans.

CHAPTER 5

Building Principles

Tactical diagramming is much like a process called "reverse engineering" whereby engineers take a piece of machinery apart to see how it works. In the same manner, a tactician mentally dissects a building to see how it might look inside. While training as an architectural engineer or contractor would certainly be helpful, it is not necessary to go to such lengths. Nevertheless, some understanding of building principles is required if for no other reason than recognizing the significance of architectural features and how they can be used to predict floor plans.

Building Basics

The most fundamental principle of building construction is that all buildings were built to serve a purpose. This is a critical point because how a building is used will directly impact its design. Two buildings that are identical on the outside will have different floor plans if they serve different purposes. A building designed for retail sales will have a different floor plan than one designed for manufacturing. Likewise, those designed for storage, agriculture or repairs will use floor plans that best suit their individual needs. Moreover, a building built for one purpose and used for another will almost always be adapted to some extent to facilitate the new use. In tactical diagramming, this principle especially works to our advantage because our focus is on residential construction and all houses are designed for people. Consequently, residential dimensions are inextricably linked to human dimensions. Besides the locations of rooms and walls, this aspect makes everything from the size of doors and windows to the width of hallways, to the height of tables and light switches, even the lengths of beds and sofas, highly predictable. A short browse through any Sears or J.C. Penney retail catalog will confirm this, as standard sizes of bed sheets, mattresses, drapes and curtains, seat cushion covers, and even furniture may change in style or color but share the same basic dimensions with similar items.

A second basic principle, introduced in the previous chapter, is that all buildings attempt to control four elements: fire, wind, water and gravity. You'll recall that gravity has a strong influence on how buildings are designed and constructed because ultimately it is the determining factor in how large an area can be spanned and how a building must be braced and built. Wind, too, can put constraints on the size, shape, location and orientation of larger buildings, though this is not usually a concern for residences. Another consideration is fire: to a greater or lesser extent, all buildings, and especially houses, are designed both to prevent fires and to provide safe exits when one occurs. Many of the regulations relating to building construction are a direct result of fire hazards. In spite of the hazards, there are "friendly fires" inside houses too. These are the fires used for heating, cooking and even entertainment. Knowing the location of a stove or fireplace provides strong indicators for identifying a kitchen, family room or master bedroom. Finally, the way an architect or builder deals with precipitation, groundwater and plumbing provides strong clues to the interior design and will be discussed in detail throughout this book.

Three Parts of a House

At the risk of oversimplification, houses can be divided into three major sections. The first is the living area. **Living areas** are where we spend most of our time while awake. They are where we greet and entertain visitors, watch television, play games or participate in other leisure-time activities. Living areas are comprised of rooms like the living room, family room, den or home office. The rooms in the living area are typically the largest in a house.

The second section is the sleeping area. While this hardly needs explanation, depending on the size and expense of a house, **sleeping areas** may consist only of bedrooms or they may also contain a master bath, a sitting room, a dressing room, and so forth. Last is the **food preparation area**. This area is where food is stored, prepared, served and eaten. It consists of the kitchen, dining room and/or breakfast nook, and pantry.

These three areas will exist in some form in every dwelling,[1] but there are other rooms that don't neatly fit into any of the three sections. Bathrooms, for example, will be found in both living and sleeping areas,[2] and closets will be found in all three areas. In fact, some walk-in closets can be large enough to be considered rooms in and of themselves. Laundry rooms are typically found near the kitchen (food preparation) but might just as appropriately be considered as part of the living area. Hallways and stairways may not be considered as rooms per se, but can be as big as any room and present formidable tactical challenges. Consequently, in order to predict a tactically useful floor plan you will require some idea of where these are.

The important thing to remember for tactical diagramming is that the rooms comprising each of these sections are almost always contiguous with each other. That is to say, all the rooms for each section tend

---

1. Nowadays, some of the nicer hotels are also including a coffee nook, refrigerator or small microwave (food preparation) and even a sitting room (living room) as part of their accommodations.
2. For many years building codes forbade bathrooms in a food preparation area. While the prohibition has for the most part been lifted, the custom remains and it is still unusual to have a bathroom adjacent to a food preparation area.

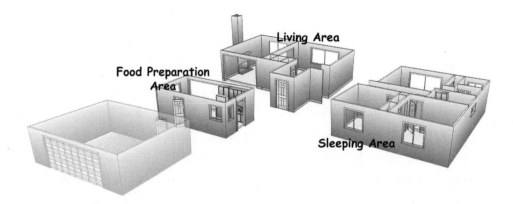

Figure 5.1 Three Parts of a House: In this view our house is broken into its three major components. Even a rudimentary ability to identify the components of a house has tactical significance because where people spend their time is largely dependent upon the time of day. During waking hours, for example, we tend to congregate in the living and food preparation area, but later at night we move to the sleeping area.

to be next to each other and not separated by rooms designed for other purposes. Thus one of the first steps in dividing a house into a floor plan is to identify these three areas. This can be done with a high degree of reliability based on the size and shape of the windows, the location of roof vents, the relationships between the windows and the vents, and other identifiable architectural features.

Spans

The **post and lintel** method of construction is one of the oldest construction techniques and can be reliably dated to as far back as 500 B.C.E. Even though the more modern term is **post and beam**, the method has not changed in thousands of years. It is simply a horizontal framing member (the lintel, more often called a beam) supported by two or more vertical framing members called posts. It would be safe to guess that there is not a single house in existence that doesn't have this structure somewhere in it. The most conspicuous place to see it is usually in a patio or a porch where the posts support a visible beam.

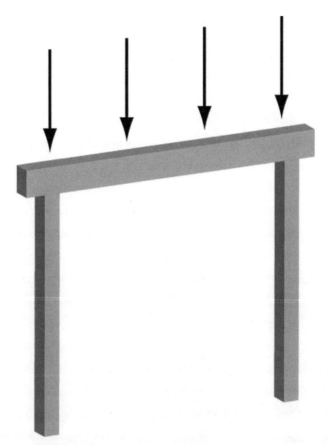

Figure 5.2 Post and Lintel Method: The oldest and simplest method of construction is called the post and lintel method and has been in continuous use for 2,500 years. All that is required is to support a lintel (beam) across two posts. The arrows depict where the load is supported.

But it is also used throughout a house in less conspicuous places, such as inside walls or under floors, to support weight across doorways and windows (in which case the beam is usually called a **header**), or even supporting an entire house with beams and short posts holding up floor joists.

When it comes to diagramming a house, this method has at least one aspect that is of particular importance. This is because there is a limit to the distance that can be spanned. While the vertical posts can support huge amounts of weight, such is not the case with horizontal beams, so weight must be distributed across a space to the vertical framing members that support it. In wood frame construction, building codes will generally require at least one inch of material for each foot of span required to support a load, but will not allow less than a 4-inch beam under any circumstances. Thus all but the widest hallways and doorways in residential construction can use a 4 x 6 or two 2 x 6s[3] on edge.

This concept becomes significant for tactical diagramming because the length of a structurally sound span is a function not only of design but of building material. Steel beams cost more than wooden ones, bigger boards cost more than smaller ones, and there is an informal standard of using the least expensive method and material because houses are almost always built as cheaply as possible. This brings us to the Cardinal Rule of Contracting: *The ability to overcome construction design difficulties is in direct proportion to the amount of money a builder is willing to spend.* Arguably, physics is not the greatest deterrent to construction obstacles—money is! If you've got the money, a contractor can almost always find a way to build it how you want it. While this sounds a little facetious, in practice it means luxury houses will be more difficult to diagram than cheaper ones.

Wood Frame Construction

About eight of ten houses in the United States[4] are of wood frame construction. This means that, regardless of what the siding and roofing may be, the framework that actually supports the structure is made from wood. Even houses that appear to be made solely from bricks, masonry, stone or concrete are almost always set over a wood frame.

The oldest form of wood frame construction in the United States

---

3. This is a nominal measurement in that modern "2 x 6s" are actually 1-1/2 x 5-1/2 inches.
4. While this book is intended for an American audience with tactical interests, much of the information is applicable in other countries. For example, while the techniques may vary somewhat, the three types of frame construction can be found in nearly every other country.

is **timber frame** construction.[5] Timber is defined as any lumber, the least dimension of which is 5 inches or greater. In the days when large timbers were plentiful, saw mills were scarce and nails were made by hand, this method of construction was practical. Timber frame construction is characterized by the use of large, widely spaced, load-bearing timbers. These large framing members are capable of supporting a lot of weight and can be spaced much further apart than the more modern 2 x 4 studs. They require few nails, sometimes none at all. Originally they were fastened together with wooden pegs, but nowadays they use heavy metal brackets and large machine bolts. Log cabins are one example of timber frame construction, as are many barns. Few modern houses use this method, however, because timber frame houses are difficult to erect, expensive to design, and provide no great advantage over the more modern **"stick framing."**[6]

When nails could be machine-made and saw mills lowered the cost of standardized sawn lumber, stick framing became the norm. This

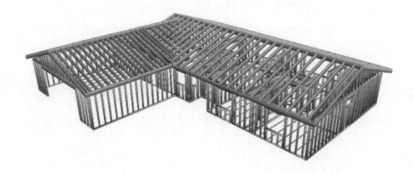

Figure 5.3 Stick Framing: Stick framing, so called because the framing members are not thicker than 2 inches, is not only the most common method of residential construction in the United States, but many other parts of the world.

---

5. Also referred to as braced frame, barn frame or eastern frame contruction, this method is still used, especially in Central Europe.
6. Stick framing takes its name from the long, slender framing members that conform to standard shapes.

method requires that no framing member be more than 2 inches thick, so nails can be driven as fasteners. This innovation revolutionized the housing industry and made buildings much easier and more economical to build.

There are two common methods of stick framing, **balloon** and **platform**. The older balloon frame method gets its name from the fact that, regardless of the number of stories, the studs run in an unbroken line from the bottom sill to the top plate. This results in a frame like a membrane or balloon with channels between the studs from the bottom to the top of the structure. It was pretty much the standard throughout most of the nineteenth century and well into the twentieth century because it compensated for green lumber shrinkage. When lumber dries, it shrinks as much as 8 percent in width but almost none in length. Since the critical dimensions of houses are usually in length, the shrinkage cracks in the stucco and plaster wall coverings are minimized with this method.

The most modern and scientific framing method yet devised is called platform framing[7] because each story is built as a separate and largely independent platform. This type of construction requires less skill and is more economical than the other types since the advent of plywood, drywall and other forms of paneling reduced the effects of lumber shrinkage even further. Consequently, this type of framing has been the most widely used for the last 50 or 60 years, and virtually all the mass-produced tract homes use this method.

Walls

For diagramming purposes, there are two types of walls. Those that support a load are called **bearing walls**, short for load-bearing walls. The other type is called a **partition** because it is used only for dividing

---

7. It is also called western framing because it is especially prevalent on the West Coast of the United States.

a building into rooms and provides no structural advantage. For this reason, partitions are more difficult to locate because they are placed largely at the discretion of the designer.

Typical loads supported by walls will be the ceiling, the floors above it (including the furniture and people), the roof, and ultimately what is on the roof, including water, ice and snow. This weight can be considerable, especially with multiple floors and tile roofs. Consequently, each bearing wall on a lower floor is virtually always directly underneath a corresponding wall above it so that the load is transferred through the strong vertical framing members (studs) directly to the foundation. This is a critical building concept because transferring a load over a space will require additional support or else the horizontal framing members will sag. This method is used regardless of the number of floors. This can be easily illustrated when viewing large buildings because the windows and doors will line up with one another from bottom to top.[8]Accordingly, strong clues for the floor plan of one story can be obtained from those above and below it.

Bearing walls provide still more clues for tactical diagramming because they support ceiling joists. Ceiling joists are normally 2 x 6s or 2 x 8s but can be as large as 2 x 14s if necessary, especially if they also serve as floor joists for an upper story. Most residential ceilings have drywall nailed to the underside of ceiling joists, and the joists must be capable of supporting the drywall, attic insulation, contents[9] and so forth, across the room without sagging. The larger the room (span), the more weight that must be supported. This can be achieved by either increasing the size of the ceiling joists or decreasing the distance between them. Neither of these choices is particularly appealing to our economically inclined residential designers and builders. Consequently,

---

8. This is called the Window Alignment Rule: *With few exceptions, windows are installed from the top down and over one another.*
9. Besides storage, many attics contain heaters, air conditioners, vents and the like.

they customarily locate interior bearing walls close enough together to support ceiling joists to avoid using larger materials or more of them. This practice provides another diagramming rule called the Rule of 14, which states: *When the width of a house or wing of a house exceeds 14 feet, suspect the presence of an interior wall.* In fact, the more the width exceeds 14 feet, the greater the likelihood of an interior wall.

Partitions are much more difficult to locate with any degree of

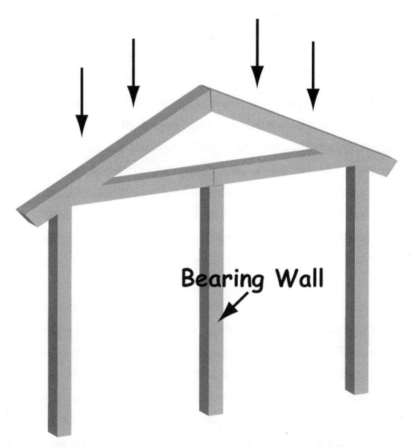

Figure 5.4 Bearing Wall: A "bearing wall" is one that supports a load. In this illustration, the bearing wall is supporting not only the weight of the roof and what is on it (the arrows on top) but the ceiling joists. Note the joint sitting on top of the bearing wall. Bearing walls are significant to tactical diagramming because their location is also more predictable than partition walls and is difficult to change for remodeling because of the continued need to support the load.

precision because they serve only to separate rooms inside a building. Nevertheless, some useful generalizations can be made. First, most building codes will not allow any habitable room in a residence except kitchens to be less than 7 feet in any dimension.[10] Kitchens are usually about 120 square feet. Second, the bathrooms of a house tend to be smaller than kitchens, most being about 100 square feet. As you will learn later in the book, kitchens and bathrooms are relatively easily identified. Third, the largest rooms in a house are usually in the living area, followed by the sleeping area. Living rooms can easily run to 300 square feet and larger, while family rooms are usually about 240 square feet. Fourth, most building codes require bedrooms to be at least 70 square feet and have at least one window that opens directly to the outside for a fire escape. In practice, however, even small bedrooms of most modern homes are rarely this small. They are almost always at least 90 square feet, and 110 square feet is nearer the norm. While these dimensions are estimates, they provide some idea of sizes that can be used in combination with other building attributes to make a highly accurate prediction of where partitions might be located.

The process of determining floor plans begins and ends with an understanding of the characteristics necessary to predict where interior walls are located. The simplest approach begins by determining where bearing walls must be, and continues by predicting where partitions are likely to be. As you proceed throughout the book, other building components, such as roof shapes, exterior doors, windows, chimneys, balconies, vents and many others, will provide more clues. Your ability to determine the floor plans of buildings will largely depend on your skill in recognizing and understanding the purpose and significance of each of these features.

---

10. Some codes, like the New York State Building Code, require at least 10 feet.

CHAPTER 6

Roofs

Roofs so quickly catch your eye, they are a design feature that can dramatically change the appearance of a house. Because of this fact, tract homes, which commonly use the same or similar floor plans, often change the shape of the roof to avoid the appearance of replication. Like a hat on a head, roofs provide protection from the elements and conceal what's underneath. In fact, if it were possible to remove this one building component, our problems with tactical diagramming would be instantly solved. However, roofs, and the features located on roofs, provide some very strong indicators for where the interior walls are located beneath them.

Roof Profiles

Roofs are always slanted to shed snow, ice or water. Even "flat" roofs are slightly inclined to allow water to drain. The amount they slope is called the "pitch" and is expressed as the number of inches of vertical rise per foot—the greater the rise, the steeper the slope. For residences, this may vary from a 3/12 to a 12/12 pitch, meaning that the roof rises from 3 to 12 inches for every 12 inches of horizontal distance. Houses built where snow and ice load is not a problem commonly use a flatter 3/12 or 4/12 pitch because these roofs use less material and are much easier to work on. This also results in a smaller attic where the air becomes heated and radiates into the living portions of the residence. In the midwestern and northeastern parts of the country a steeper pitch is often preferred because it sheds snow and ice more quickly and easily.

While steep roofs may shed snow and ice, they also create a large space underneath. Once again, our frugal builders and designers want to leave nothing to waste and frequently use this space as a living area. This brings us to the 45 Rule: *Whenever a roof has a pitch of 45°[1] or greater, suspect the presence of a living space under the roof.* This space is almost always used as a sleeping area.

Like the studs, plates and soles of the walls beneath them, modern wood frame roofs use "two-bys" as structural members for all the same reasons. The framing members supporting roofs are called **rafters**, and the ceiling joists across the walls provide the horizontal framing members. Thus the most common roof configuration takes the shape of an isosceles triangle. This aspect provides a clue to the location of the walls below because of the practice of placing a bearing wall to support the ceiling joists near the center of the building under the long ridgeline of the roof. This wall is often one side of a hallway and need not be directly under the center of the roof's ridgeline or run in a perfectly straight line. But it does provide an indicator that there will be a wall somewhere in the immediate vicinity and can be used with other indicators to begin to determine the floor design.

Because triangles cannot deform without bending or breaking either the fasteners or the sides, they are the strongest geometrical shape and builders use them whenever possible to achieve maximum strength and rigidity with a minimum of material. Triangles also allow a framing component called a **truss** to be used in place of the rafters and ceiling joists. Trusses are rigid wooden frames of triangular shapes, capable of supporting both the ceiling below and the roofing above over much

---

1.   This equates to a 12/12 pitch.

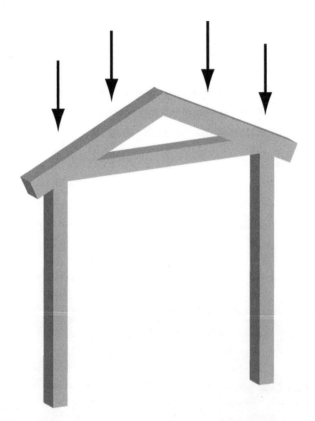

Figure 6.1 Rafter Method: When constructing roofs, the rafter method is one of the simplest and cheapest methods of distributing loads (indicted by the arrows) while allowing the roof to shed snow, ice and rain. The rafters sit on walls and are held from separating by a collar tie or ceiling joist. This creates a triangle—the strongest geometric figure because it can not be deformed. Consequently, contractors will use triangles in any number of applications.

larger spans than rafters. Because they use less material and are faster to erect than the rafter method, they have gained immense popularity in the building industry. The significance for tactical diagramming, however, is that trusses do not need an interior bearing wall. Consequently, do not assume a bearing wall in the center of the building simply because of the shape of the roof. Always attempt to confirm it by more than one feature. This brings us to the most important rule in tactical diagramming. This rule, known as the Cardinal Rule of Diagramming, states: *As the number of details you use to predict the location of inside features increases, so does the degree of reliability and precision of your diagram.* No architectural feature, regardless of how reliable it has proven to be for predicting floor plans in the past, should be considered in isolation. There are simply too many permutations in construction to ignore other clues because of a misguided overconfidence in one.

Roof Styles

Building roofs come in all shapes, sizes and colors. Many buildings

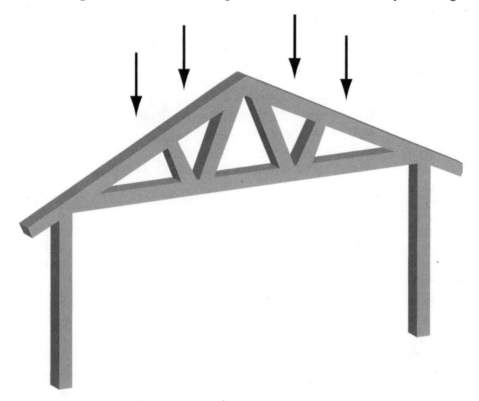

Figure 6.2 Truss Method: Like its predecessor, the rafter, trusses use triangles to gain strength and rigidity. By combining a series of triangles, smaller-sized framing members are able to span greater distances. This reduces, and often eliminates, the need for an intermediate bearing wall. Trusses substitute for rafters and are almost always assembled off site. As manufacturing processes have become more modern, trusses have become more popular.

use more than one style. Each style of roof has advantages and disad-vantages, but two are predominant for American houses. These are the gable roof and the hip roof, followed closely by the shed roof. In fact, most of the other roof styles are simply variations of these three. The following is a list of the various roofing styles in the general order they are preferred by American homeowners.

Gable Roofs—The most popular roof style for housing in the United States is the gable roof. This style is economical, easy to erect, and pro-vides space for an attic. It is built with two sloping sides that meet at the ridge near the middle and terminate at the end walls of the house. The triangular space that connects the wall with the roof at the ends of the house is called the gable, which is where the name comes from. Gable roofs can vary in pitch, but the steeper they are the more likely the space underneath them will be used for a living space (normally as a sleeping

Figure 6.3 Gable Roof: The most popular roof style in the United States is the gable roof. It is economical, easy to erect, and provides space under the roof for storage, and in some cases even sleeping.

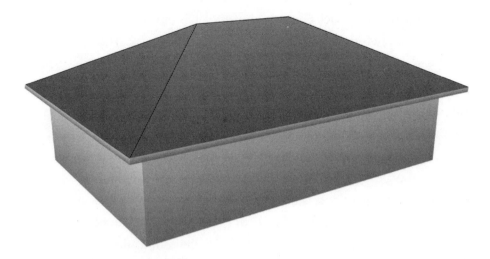

Figure 6.4 Hip Roof: The second most popular roof style in the United States is the hip roof. Hip roofs have the gables "tipped in" to form part of the roof. Many houses use a combination of gable and hip styles in the same building.

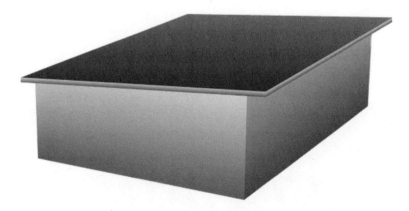

Figure 6.5 Shed and Flat Roof: Shed and flat roofs will often cover patios, porches, carports, garages and outlying buildings. For diagramming purposes they may be considered identical because they require the same underlying support.

area) rather than storage. Observing a window in the gable is an especially strong indicator (see the section on dormers, below).

Hip Roofs—The hip roof is a variation of the gable roof with the primary difference that the gables are "tipped in" to form part of the roof. Some square roofs have the gables tipped clear to the center, forming a four-sided pyramid. Except in some of the larger and more luxurious houses, hip roofs are seldom steeper than a 4/12 pitch and almost never have a living space under them because of the reduced headroom. Probably because they are harder to build than gable roofs and have reduced head room, they are not as popular on two-story homes. One major advantage of hip roofs is that they tend to stand up better in high-wind areas, especially where hurricanes and tornadoes are prevalent.

Shed and Flat Roofs—While not as common as gable or hip roofs, they are often found in combination with other styles. Many times they will cover porches, patios, carports or garages that are attached to a larger structure with a different roof style. For diagramming purposes, about the only difference between shed and flat roofs is that shed roofs have a steeper pitch. This means that vents coming through the roof are virtually diagnostic for locating a wall underneath because of the difficulty in "stacking" vents in buildings without attics.[2]

Gambrel (Barn) Roofs—This roof has been used so often for barns that it is often called the "barn roof" and is extremely easy to recognize. While among the most difficult to construct, gambrel roofs have the advantage of providing a large space under the roof without increasing the height of the building. Gambrel roofs are not as common as either gable or hip roofs but are popular where zoning requirements limit the height of buildings. For diagramming purposes, the space under a gambrel roof of a residence should be considered as a second story and is almost always used as a sleeping area.

---

2. For information on stacked vents, see Chapter 7.

Figure 6.6 Gambrel Roof: The proper name for the so-called "barn roof" is the gambrel roof. Despite their nickname, gambrel roofs are often used for dwellings and the space under the roof is nearly always used for a sleeping area.

Figure 6.7 Monitor Roof: One advantage in tactical diagramming of the monitor roof is that the center bearing wall is always exposed. Even so, aerial photographs are usually necessary because the higher roof is used to hide vents, solar panels, air conditioning units and the like. The center wall between the two roof lines is also commonly used for windows. Another use is to have the higher roof line hide appliances such as air conditioners, turbine vents, solar heating panels and the like.

Figure 6.8 Mansard Roof: As with the gambrel roof style, the living space directly under the roof is used for a sleeping area. Dormers anywhere in this style of roof should be considered conclusive proof.

Monitor Roofs—This style of roof is similar in appearance to a gable roof except that the two sides of the roof do not meet at the ridgeline. One side, almost always the south side or the side away from the front of the house, is several feet lower than the other. The space between the two roof ridges is used for windows, skylights or solar panels. This style is becoming increasingly popular, especially in luxury homes, because vents can be stacked and hidden from the front of the location and/or windows are installed to provide natural lighting. When the space is used for solar panels, the south side is preferred because it is never in shadow.[3] The best way to detect this style of roof is with aerial photographs because the lower roof side is usually hidden by the front.

---

3. This is true for the Northern Hemisphere only.

Mansard (French) Roofs—The mansard roof is sometimes called a French roof and takes its name from François Mansart, the French architect who designed it. These roofs are seldom found on American homes but can often be seen in small commercial and retail buildings. Homes that use this style are generally large Victorian dwellings constructed late in the nineteenth or very early twentieth centuries. They are similar to gambrel (barn) roofs with the gable turned in toward the center in the same manner as a hip roof. Thus it has eight sloping sides, four near vertical lower sides and four near flat upper sides. Like the gambrel style, mansard roofs provide a large space under the roof without increasing the height of the building and are appealing where zoning ordinances limit the height of buildings.

Roof Color and Texture

Roofs are covered with a number of materials, including tile, slate, copper, aluminum, asphalt or wooden shingles or shakes. Roofing is very expensive, and material and installation can easily cost a building owner upwards of $5,000. As a result, reroofing an entire structure is often prohibitively expensive. All of the above materials, to a greater or lesser extent, deteriorate and fade with age and exposure to the elements. Because additions and modifications often require a new roof or partial replacement of an existing roof, the difference in colors, even when using identical materials, is usually highly conspicuous. Recognizing additions and remodeling is especially important in tactical diagramming because they do not always follow building codes and practices as closely as the rest of the house. When diagramming a building, especially a residence, any difference in roof color, texture or material is a strong clue that the building was not all constructed at the same time.[4]

---

4. For information on additions, see Chapter 11.

Attics

An attic is a story or room directly below the roof of a building, especially a house. For most houses, a single, undivided attic covering the entire house is the norm. In the same manner, multiple-dwelling buildings, such as apartments, condominiums, motels and the like, have separate living spaces that share a common attic. This is particularly important in tactical operations because suspects frequently climb into attics to avoid detection, seek an escape route or find a clean air source when tear gas is introduced. Consequently, when diagramming these types of locations, it is important to remember that a suspect can climb out of one living area and into another. When attics exceed 3,000 square feet, most building codes require separations similar to the walls below.[5]

Typically attics are not intended for habitation because they lack the necessary headroom clearance required by most building codes. This problem is often overcome with the use of dormers (see following section) or by simply using the center of the building. Even so, most building codes will require at least 50 percent of the usable area to be at least 7'6" and no portion to be less than 5 feet in height. Consequently, when houses use attics for sleeping areas, look for closets near the eaves of the house.

Dormers

Dormers are framed structures that project from a roof surface and add space, light and ventilation to an attic area. They generally come in two styles, the gable dormer and the shed dormer. Some homes will use both, with one or more gable dormers in the front and a shed dormer in the

---

5. While 3,000 square feet is the norm, attics constructed of noncombustible materials or equipped with sprinklers may remain undivided up to as large as 9,000 square feet.

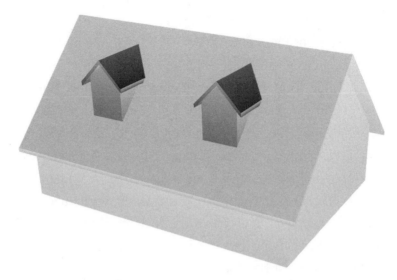

Figure 6.9 Dormer, Gable: Dormers are small appendages jutting out from roofs. They are used for both aesthetic and practical reasons. The gable dormer is so called because it uses a gable roof style.

back. Shed dormers are larger than gable dormers and may stretch nearly across the entire building.

Some dormers are decorative in nature and may be used only for aesthetic reasons and/or to provide attic ventilation. With rare exceptions, however, the additional attic headroom created by dormers is almost always used as a sleeping area. In fact, the word "dormer" comes from the French *dormir*, which means "to sleep." When diagramming, the presence of any dormer in a roof should cause a strong suspicion of a sleeping area, particularly a bedroom. In fact, if the dormer has a window, it is nearly certain, hence the Dormer Window Rule, which states: *Windows in dormers or gables are strong indicators of living or sleeping areas above the first floor.*

Skylights

Skylights are becoming increasingly popular. They are almost always rectangular and not more than 24 inches wide to allow them to fit

Figure 6.10 Dormer, Shed: Like its fraternal twin, the gable dormer, the shed dormer takes its name from the roof style. Dormers of either type should immediately arouse suspicion of a sleeping area under the roof, especially if the dormers contain windows.

between rafters and trusses. While they can be wider, this method requires additional framing and makes them more expensive. For tactical diagramming, skylights are important not so much for predicting where interior walls might be but rather for indicating where they *cannot* be, because they are never placed over interior walls.

Like windows in walls, skylights are most often placed in the middle of the ceiling of a room for aesthetic reasons. When more than one is used, they are frequently placed in alternating rafter spaces and provide light for the same room. When skylights are used with other architectural features, their location provides an indication of where interior walls might be if you estimate the distance between the likely place for a wall (interior or exterior) and then add the distance to the other side of the skylight.[6] From time to time there will be a series of skylights with only a short space between them. When this design is used, measure

---

6. For more information on this method, see "Window Analysis" in Chapter 9.

the distance to a known wall and add the distance to the entire series of skylights to predict the interior wall. This technique should always be used in conjunction with other features, such as vents and windows, to increase precision and reliability because the placement of skylights can be highly individualistic.

Nearly Useless Features

Every feature on a building serves a purpose, even if it is only an aesthetic purpose. Nevertheless, not all features are useful for tactical diagramming. To avoid becoming confused by other, seemingly important architectural features on roofs, it will be useful to recognize some of those that can safely be ignored.

Solar heating panels seldom provide information useful for tactical diagramming. They are commonly placed on the south side of a roof to obtain maximum exposure to the sun and as close to the water heater as is practical so that the hot water can be stored and insulated and ready for use. Nevertheless, the pipes that connect these panels to a water heater can be some distance from the water heater because they are commonly insulated and the placement of the solar panels to gather sunlight and heat is more critical than the distance to the water heater. Consequently, solar panels are nearly useless for providing clues to interior floor plans but may be used to orient aerial photographs or as a navigation aid for tactical team members because of the practice of always placing them on the south side of the house.

The size of the roof overhangs (eaves) is also of little use. In the colder climates, overhangs are almost nonexistent to allow the sun maximum exposure to the exterior walls for passive heating. In the hotter climates, particularly in the southern and southwestern portions of the United States, overhangs frequently exceed two feet and more. This is to provide shade to avoid heating the walls. Neither style has any particular significance for tactical diagramming.

When viewing aerial photographs, some of the most conspicuous features on a roof are satellite television dishes and antennas. While lead-in wires may provide some clues as to the type of room,[7] they should always be viewed with suspicion because of the ease of moving the wire inside the attic to remote locations inside the building.

While roof vents are covered in detail in the next chapter, it is appropriate to mention here that only two types are useful for determining floor plans. These are those that serve water appliances, such as showers, bathrooms and sinks, and those that serve combustion appliances, such as water heaters, furnaces and central heaters. Other vents, such as ridge vents, gable vents, air conditioning ducts, stove vents, and turbine vents, are of marginal value.

---

7.   Usually a living room, family room or master bedroom.

CHAPTER 7

Vents and Ducts

Vents are normally found on roofs, and logically the chapter on roofs would be the place to describe their significance. Vents provide so many clues for tactical diagramming, however, that they deserve an entire chapter for themselves. You probably never thought of vents as being useful for determining floor plans because they are not very conspicuous. In fact, most contractors will go to some lengths to make them as inconspicuous as possible because they are not acsthetically pleasing. Yet vents in buildings are indispensable, and even a small house can have a half-dozen or more. So why have you never noticed them? Because they are in the walls. Many, in fact, simply poke through the roof directly above the wall in which they are located. When viewing these vents on an aerial photograph, tactical diagramming becomes almost as simple as "connecting the dots."

Water Appliance Vents

Water appliance vents are those used to vent showers, toilets, sinks, tubs and other similar fixtures that require drains. Without these vents the drains would not function. This can be easily demonstrated with a drinking straw and a glass of water. When you stick the straw into the water and then place your thumb over the end you can pull the entire straw from the glass and the water will remain inside the straw. As soon as you move your finger the liquid falls from the straw. This same principle requires that air be allowed to enter and escape from your drain system for the drains to function properly.

Water appliance vents are almost always the smallest vents on a roof. For residential construction, they most often consist of a 1-1/2- inch[1] PVC or galvanized pipe sticking through the roof about 6 to 8 inches. In colder climates, where they might be plugged by snow, they are often larger in diameter and a minimum of 10 inches above the roof, but it is not uncommon to find them rising a foot or more. These vents have no caps since there is no need to keep rain out. In fact, they connect

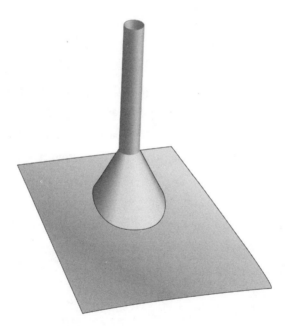

Figure 7.1 Water Appliance Vent: Water appliance vents can be distinguished by their small size, the style of flashing around them and the fact that they have no cap. They are normally painted to match the roof color but sometimes match the color of the trim.

---

1. Pipe is measured with an inside diameter. Consequently, a vent pipe with a 1-1/2-inch diameter is nearly 2 inches in outside diameter.

directly into a drain and any rain that falls inside them is simply drained with the waste water. They are, however, common sources of leaks in roofs because water can run down the outside of the vent pipe into the structure. To avoid this, the vents are equipped with a flashing that fits tightly against the pipe, often with a rubber or plastic collar, and tapers sharply on the high side of the roof and then much more gradually on the lower side. Because the bottom half of the flashing always remains on the top of the roofing material to allow water to drain off, it is sometimes easier to identify than the vent itself.

Water appliance vents are usually painted the same color as the roofing material to make them as inconspicuous as possible, so it requires close observation to spot them. Less commonly, vents may be painted the same color as the house trim. This makes them much easier to notice, but even then their small size makes them difficult to identify in all but the clearest photographs. One of the best methods for detecting these small vents is with the use of aerial photographs, especially those taken in the early morning or late evening hours when the sun is low on the horizon. At these times, a vent casts shadows that are more noticeable than the vent.

Sometimes there may be several of these vents in a row. When this occurs it is one of the few architectural features that is virtually diagnostic in that there is a near certainty that an interior wall is directly underneath. Furthermore, you can be pretty sure that there is no door in the portion of the wall under the row of vents. This is because of the construction problems of routing pipes around an opening as big as a door.

This building practice is also helpful when diagramming a multiple-story building because building designers and contractors will try to use the same vent for more than one appliance on more than one floor, so the vent will continue upward in a straight line through more than one story. This is of tremendous advantage since the upper stories obscure many of the architectural features you would ordinarily use to determine the floor plan of the first floor.

Figure 7.2 Vent in a Wall: Because water appliance vents are easily concealed inside walls, they often protrude directly through the roof above the wall. Consequently, they provide strong indicators of interior walls beneath them.

Generally, each water appliance vent pipe will indicate a water appliance. There is one exception to this rule, however. Builders will often run several vents together and have one larger vent pipe extend through the roof rather than a number of smaller ones. This system is called a stack vent system.[2] Sometimes a builder will use a stack vent to move all the vents to the rear of the house for aesthetic reasons. When

_____

2. Sometimes called a common vent system.

this practice is used, it greatly diminishes the reliability of using the vent to determine the location of interior walls.[3]

To identify a stack vent system, look at the size and number of water appliance vents. When a stack vent system is used the vent pipe will not be less than 2 inches in diameter (2-1/2 inches outside diameter) and is sometimes even larger. Stack vents are often high on the roof near the ridge to allow room in the attic to connect multiple water appliance vents. If you observe a stack vent low on the roof (near the eaves), it remains a good indicator that it is over an interior wall. While a stack vent system may preclude the precise identification of interior walls, it may be used in conjunction with other features such as windows, doors and other vents to identify the type of area within the house and sometimes the purpose of the rooms underneath.

A good rule of thumb is the Multiple Vent Rule. Simply put, this says: *The more vents sticking through a roof, the more likely an interior wall is directly beneath them.* This is especially so when observing water appliance vents, because when a builder uses a stack vent there are fewer vents. Therefore, the more water appliance vents you observe, the less likely it is that they are part of a stack vent system, especially when they are in close proximity to each other. Another strong indicator is the size of the vent pipes. Stack vents require larger pipes. Hence, a lack of larger-diameter vents is another indicator that each of the vents you observe represents a separate water appliance underneath as well as an interior wall that hides the plumbing.[4]

The reliability of a wall existing directly under a vent also rises considerably when the vent is located in an area where the roof is near the

---

3. Stack vents on multi-story buildings are more reliable than when observed on one-story buildings because of a building practice of locating water appliances underneath one another to allow the passage of vents through walls in upper stories.
4. Builders frequently use stack vents where practical and single-appliance vents elsewhere. Consequently, observing a stack vent system will not preclude single-appliance vents at other places in the same roof.

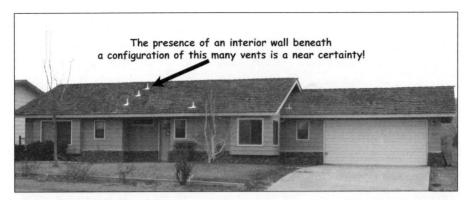

The presence of an interior wall beneath a configuration of this many vents is a near certainty!

Figure 7.3 Vents in a Row: Because water appliance vents are easily concealed inside walls, they often protrude directly through the roof. Consequently, they provide strong indicators of interior walls beneath them.

ceiling. On shallow gable and hip roofs this means near the eaves where the slope of the roof is usually within 1 or 2 feet of the ceiling under it. This is because of the lack of room between the ceiling and the roof for the builder to move the vent. Pipe, even plastic pipe, doesn't bend very easily, and building codes require all water appliance vents to continue upward with no sags, dips or drops. When a builder uses a stack vent to connect a number of vents, he most often extends the stack vent upward toward the ridge of the roof to gain enough height to allow room for the fittings of the additional individual vents. Thus, two more diagramming rules are revealed. The Perimeter Vent Rule states: *When a roof vent is not in an exterior wall, the closer it is located to the edge of the roof, the more likely there is an interior wall beneath it.* The second rule of thumb is called the Limited Option Rule, which states: *Vents extending through shed and flat roofs are strong indicators of an interior wall beneath them.* This rule is applicable regardless of where the vents are observed in the roof, but the flatter the roof, the more certain you can be of a wall beneath them. Both of these rules are dependent upon the fact that there is simply not enough room to move the vents and so the simplest method is to continue the vertical run through the roof.

One caveat with vent rules in general pertains to precisely locating the wall below the vents. This is because of a common building practice of plumbers and framers[5] pushing a vent pipe to one side of a rafter or truss to avoid additional framing. While pipes don't easily bend, even steel pipe can be leaned to some extent, and when pipes are directly underneath a rafter or truss it is much easier to push them to the side than to frame around them. This practice may mean that the top of the vent pipe poking through the roof will be off the center of the wall beneath it by several inches or as much as a foot. This is almost never tactically significant, since predicting an interior wall within 1 foot of its actual location is much more precision than is usually necessary. Remember, we're trying to build a reliable floor plan, not a set of blueprints.

Combustion Vents

Combustion vents provide a means to exhaust carbon monoxide and other toxic vapors for appliances that use fire in some manner. Examples of combustion appliances are central heating, furnaces, stoves and water heaters.[6] Combustion vents are usually the largest vents on a roof and the easiest to recognize because of their high profile. Depending upon when the house was built, they may be clay pipe, asbestos, double steel wall or even triple steel wall. They are usually 6 inches or more in diameter and stick up from the roof 2 feet or more. Furthermore, all combustion vents have caps. The caps vary somewhat in appearance but are designed to allow hot gases to escape while keeping rain and snow out. The caps are usually cylindrical and 2 to 4 inches larger in diameter than the vent pipe, although they are sometimes oval or dome-shaped. In addition to caps, combustion vents often have storm collars. A storm

---

5. A framer is a builder who specializes, sometimes exclusively, in erecting only the structure of the building.
6. In some parts of the country, these appliances may be electric. Electrical appliances do not require combustion vents.

collar works like an umbrella. It is simply a sloping ring positioned just above the roof flashing. When the vent gets rained on, the water runs down the outside of the vent pipe until it reaches the storm collar, where it is diverted away and allowed to drip on the roof. This prevents water from running down the vent and damaging the appliance, which is particularly important for combustion appliances.

While combustion vents will not provide information about interior walls with the assurance and precision of water appliance vents, they are still useful for tactical diagramming. For instance, it is of particular advantage to identify the combustion vent that serves the water heater. The water heater is nearly always located within 25 feet of the kitchen sink because of the high demand for hot water in the kitchen. While showers also use hot water, people are willing to wait for a warm shower or bath but want hot water immediately in the kitchen. This has resulted in a building practice of placing the hot water heater near the kitchen.[7]

Locating the kitchen is especially important in diagramming a house for two reasons. The first is that it is one of the two most common places suspects go to dispose of evidence, particularly drugs.[8] The second reason is that once the kitchen of a dwelling can be identified, other adjacent rooms, such as dining rooms, pantries and breakfast areas, are more noticeable because they are nearly always collocated with the kitchen.

There are two common locations to begin looking for the combustion vent serving the water heater. In newer construction, the attached garage is the first place to start looking. The water heater is usually placed against the wall closest to the kitchen on a 2-foot platform. The hot water in the tank has a short distance to travel and allows the small amount of tepid or cool water in the pipe to run out quickly. Should the pilot light be blown out, the heavier-than-air gaseous fuel will flow off

---

7. Larger and more luxurious homes may have more than one water heater.
8. The other common location is a bathroom.

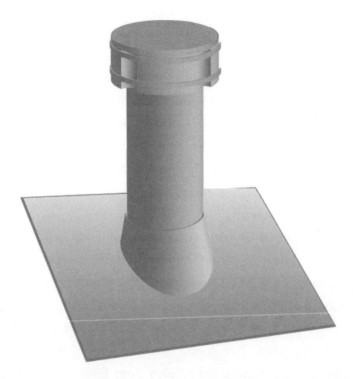

Figure 7.4 Combustion Vent: Combustion vents are the largest on a roof, often 6 inches or more in diameter and several feet tall. They are characterized by a cap to keep water out and serve appliances that require combustion, such as the furnace and water heater.

the platform and away from the pilot light and reduce the likelihood of a fire. Furthermore, a fire in the garage may help limit the damage by providing more time for detection and allowing the occupants to flee. In older construction the water heater is often located outside the house in a ventilated closet or separate compartment that is accessed from an outside door.

Another common combustion vent is that of the central heating appliance. Furnaces are often located near the center of the house because of the need for circulating hot air. The farther the air has to travel, the more difficult it is to "push" and keep warm. In more modern homes, furnaces may also be located in basements, attics, walls and attached garages.

When the building you wish to diagram is suspected of having more than one dwelling inside, look for more than one heating or furnace vent. To accommodate personal preferences, each dwelling will usually have its own furnace. When these are located next to one another, they usually indicate a reverse floor plan.[9] When more than one furnace vent can be identified in a building you may be able to identify what at first glance appears to be a house but is actually a multiple dwelling, such as a townhouse or condominium. This has substantial tactical significance since each dwelling will require independent probable cause, and usually its own search warrant.

Before moving on to other vents, one additional combustion vent with tactical significance should be mentioned. Chimneys are the oldest form of combustion vent and are still used extensively in some parts of the country. The style people are most familiar with is the masonry chimney, which is most commonly constructed of bricks or blocks but may also be constructed of rocks. Masonry chimneys are extremely expensive and consequently have fallen from favor as less expensive methods have become available. A critical point for tactical diagramming is that masonry chimneys must always be placed on concrete footings. This means that even buildings that have additions or have been remodeled seldom move a masonry chimney. Consequently, the appliance that uses such a chimney, especially a fireplace, is also in the original location.

Newer construction methods have enabled "zero tolerance" fireplaces. These are simply prefabricated fireplaces that are constructed so that they can be placed in contact with wooden framing members without setting them afire when the fireplace is used. Likewise, the chimneys that service these fireplaces are no longer masonry but rather double- and triple-walled steel vents. Nevertheless, for aesthetic reasons, they

---

9. Tract homes, condominiums, apartments, motels and hotels often use a reverse floor plan. These are mirror images of each other.

are almost always enclosed in a wood frame structure that is built to resemble the older masonry chimneys and sided with "look-alike" brick or stone, or sometimes with the same material used for the house siding. Fireplaces in older houses are commonly located in the living room but in more contemporary houses may be in either a living room or a family room. If a fireplace is determined to be located in a bedroom, it is nearly always the master bedroom.

Other Vents and Ducts

Besides water appliance and combustion vents, houses have one or more exhaust vents. These vents are designed to remove things like cooking fumes, odors and water vapor from the structure. For example, a family of four typically generates more than 22 pounds of water vapor every day, and an inside clothes washer and dryer can produce 30 pounds of water vapor by itself. If this moisture is not removed from a house it can easily lead to offensive odors, mold and rot. Consequently, exhaust vents are used to remove these vapors and can also provide useful information for tactical diagramming.

Stove vents are used to exhaust cooking fumes and odors and are important in diagramming since they are often located near the kitchen range. Stove vents are often as large in diameter as combustion vents but do not have a requirement to be of any particular height above the roof. In fact, they don't even have to be on the roof at all. Many stove vents are located on an exterior kitchen wall behind the stove. When the stove vent exhausts through the roof it is often as large as 6 to 8 inches in diameter but very close to the roof. These vents always have caps, and a "roof jack" type of flashing is common. A roof jack is simply a flashing and cap built as one assembly. It is seldom more than one foot tall and appears to have a half-cylinder placed across the top for a cap.

Stove vents are most often painted the color of the roof or trim but may be detected by a dirty stain around them. This is a result of the dirt that sticks to the oily residue from the cooking fumes. Another place to look for a stove vent is on the exterior wall of the kitchen. When placed here the stove vent is usually rectangular, often with louvers, and placed just under the eaves. It is most often painted the same color as the siding of the house and may be difficult to locate. As with all vents, their shadow is often the most noticeable characteristic.

Bathrooms are also usually vented. In fact, most building codes require every full bathroom[10] to have a window of at least 3 square feet,[11] half of which must be able to be opened, or the room must be equipped with a mechanical ventilation system direct to the exterior of the building. Bathroom exhaust vents through roofs have no tactical diagramming value because they are usually flexible tubing that can be easily installed in any location. Bathroom vents through walls, however, are extremely reliable indicators.

Like bathroom vents, dryer vents most often use flexible conduit and are useful in tactical diagramming only for general location. They can usually be identified, especially in newer homes, because they are the lowest vents in the building, often right above the ground. Similarly, while they provide some predictive value as to the general location of the dryer (and washer) they provide little useful information for tactical diagramming.

Air conditioning ducts are usually large rectangular conduits often reaching dimensions of 2 feet square or more. Sometimes they may be flexible ducts and are anchored periodically to the roof. Usually there is no attempt to paint air conditioning vents on roofs. This is probably because they are treated to prevent rust when manufactured and are too big to hide anyway.

---

10. In newer and/or more luxurious houses, it is common to have toilet facilities in several areas of the house without a tub or shower. These are referred to as "half baths." At a minimum, these rooms will contain both a toilet and a sink.

11. For information on identifying bathroom windows, see Chapter 9.

Air conditioning vents and ducts are significant only on buildings with very low pitched roofs. These vents do not terminate in walls but are usually placed in the attic of the building, or occasionally right on the roof. When placed on the roof they often mean that the air conditioning was added after the building was constructed or there was not room enough to place the air conditioning ducts in the attic. This is a common building practice in light commercial construction where ease of maintenance and repairs outweigh aesthetic concerns. When installed in this manner, air conditioning ducts run along the tops of roofs and then terminate in vents inside the individual rooms. Thus the number of rooms can be estimated as well as their approximate locations. Since larger rooms require a larger amount of conditioned air, larger vents and ducts are necessary to service them. In this manner the size of the air conditioning vents can be used as an indicator.

While there are a number of other vents commonly found on a residence, such as turbine vents, ridge vents, gable vents, dormer vents, eyebrow vents and so forth, they have virtually no tactical diagramming significance.

Vent Patterns

One often-overlooked benefit of vents in tactical diagramming is their relationship with each other. For instance, multiple water appliance vents in a row provide almost conclusive evidence of an interior wall beneath them. Masonry chimneys are so difficult to move that even when additions and/or remodeling are detected, the chimney is always in the same place. While these patterns are quite conspicuous, an astute observer will notice more subtle patterns that are just as significant. The best example is the Vent Pattern Rule, which states that *any pattern of vents, regardless of their style, type, purpose or combination, that is repeated on another building, provides near conclusive evidence that the floor plans are identical.*

Figure 7.5 Vent Patterns: While these houses under construction conspicuously have the same vent pattern and floor plan, this principle works equally well when contractors "disguise" the appearance of adjacent houses to make them more appealing, a common occurrence in tract homes. Regardless of the texture, color, roof style, siding or landscaping, a shared vent pattern is indicative of common floor plans. Thus the features of one building can be used to predict the floor plan of another. The significance of this principle (Vent Pattern Rule) can be profound for tactical diagramming, especially when a "walk through" of another house will provide insight into the target location.

This is because of a common building practice, especially among tract homes, of using the same floor plan for many houses. To a novice, the homes appear dissimilar because of the ingenuity of the designer in changing the roof style, siding, landscaping and color. The floor plans, however, are identical; therefore the architectural features of one building can be used to predict the floor plan of another. The advantage this provides in gaining surreptitious tactical diagramming information requires no additional comment.

CHAPTER 8

Doors

The significance of doors for tactical diagramming is difficult to overestimate. They are usually a structure's most vulnerable component, and the main door of a building is also the most common point for forced entry. Doors reveal much of what is behind them by their style, shape, size and location. In fact, they are often used to represent an entire residence, as when someone says, "They live two doors down the street." Doors are one of only two components of a structure that must move to function, the other being windows. Doors may swing, slide, fold, revolve, rise or roll up. They can be made from wood, metal, glass, fiberglass or any combination. Doors are especially valuable for tactical diagramming because they are so closely regulated by building codes.

Every door is part of an exit system, which is why building codes so closely regulate the size, type and placement of doors, especially for occupied structures like houses, apartments, hotels, hospitals, schools and businesses. Most building codes will require any exit system to provide a continuous, unobstructed and undiminished[1] path of travel from any occupied point in a building to a public way.[2] Furthermore,

---

1. In other words, the width of the exit path cannot decrease as the path continues.
2. A public way is any street, alley or parcel of land essentially unobstructed from the ground to the sky and owned, operated or used by the public. For purposes of emergency escape, most commercial building codes require that the path of travel have a clear width of not less than 10 feet.

buildings that are only partially occupied or occupied for only part of the day will be required to meet the same standards. As a result of these regulations, a building practice has evolved to comply with them even when they are not required. This is so that if an owner wants to someday use the building for something that *will* require that these standards be met (since buildings often outlive their originally designed purpose), no major remodeling will be required. For tactical diagramming purposes, this makes the location, style and swing of doors highly predictable.

Exterior Doors

Businesses—Probably all of us have been lost in a public build-ing at least once. While this is a nuisance most of the time, it can be tragic in a fire, earthquake or other emergency. Consequently, building codes will require exit doors to be clearly marked, and in a building with an occupant load[3] of 50 or greater they must swing out toward safety. This regulation is strictly enforced and will even require ret-roactive corrections if an older building is converted for commerce or

Figure 8.1 Doors, Business: With almost no exceptions, doors for businesses swing from the building toward the outside. This is because these doors are a means of emer-gency exit and the building codes are firm and strictly enforced, so much so that the doors in many buildings comply even without being required.

---

3. The occupant load is the number of people that can be expected to use the building while it's open for business.

some similar purpose. Furthermore, it covers all exit doors, regardless of style, operation or material. Sliding doors in a grocery store and revolving doors in a fancy hotel are *not* excepted. The next time you encounter one of these types, notice a small sign either near the latch or in the lower middle of the door that states something to the effect of "In case of emergency, push firmly outward." These doors are on breakaway hinges that will release the door if forcefully pushed. If for some reason a door can't meet the requirements, a door that does must be immediately adjacent.

Most building codes will go still further and require "nonmanipulable" door locks on all primary exit doors. This simply means you do not need to use your hands to make the door open. These latches are most commonly long handles that cross the entire door and are often called panic locks because a crowd surging against them will automatically open the door.[4] And, because retrofitting increases the lease or resale expense of a building, those that even *might* be used in such a manner routinely have their exit doors designed to meet the higher standards from the outset. This practice is also a valuable tool for tactical diagramming[5] because it makes the direction the door swings more predictable, as expressed as the Public Entry/Exit Rule: *All public entry doors, and all doors available to the public, swing toward the outside of the building.*

Residences—The primary entrance in a house is often called the "front door," though this door may not always be in the front of the building anymore. While most are still on the street side of a house, they can also be found on another side, off a porch, in an alcove or even

---

4. It should be noted that while panic locks are required on primary exit doors, other doors in the emergency exit system, such those exiting to fire escapes, stairs and so forth, may use other types of latches.
5. Besides being useful for diagramming, this rule is the equivalent to an "artificial compass" since the direction an exit door swings is most likely toward the exterior of the building.

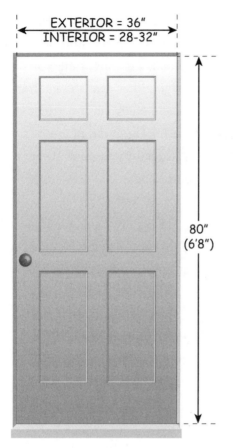

EXTERIOR = 36"
INTERIOR = 28-32"

80"
(6'8")

Figure 8-2 Doors Dimensions: Doors are one of the most highly regulated components of any building and consequently, are one of the most predictable. Regardless of whether a door is interior, exterior or used in a house or business, they are nearly always about 80 inches tall. Entrance doors are never less than 36 inches wide and cannot be more than 48 inches wide for a single leaf. If a wider opening is needed more than one leaf (double-door) is used. Interior doors are the same height and only slightly more narrow.

behind a masonry wall off a courtyard. They are easily identified, however, because they are intended to attract the attention of people to expedite access. Sidewalks, walkways, house numbers, porch lights, doorbells, door mats, mail boxes and landscaping all attempt to make this an attractive and attention-getting locale. This door, and its hardware, are easily the most expensive in a house and can easily run to several thousand dollars or more.

The main entrance door of a house is virtually always 36 inches wide, 80 inches tall and 1-3/4 inches thick. This is because most building codes will not allow the leaf of any exit door to be less than 36 inches wide or more than 48 inches wide.[6] Consequently, they are almost always 36 inches—no more, no less. These are heavy, solid-core doors that require at least three sets of hinges and are often equipped with both

---

6. This includes doors for commercial buildings as well.

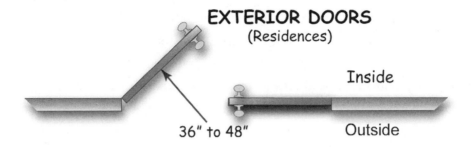

EXTERIOR DOORS
(Residences)

Inside

Outside

36" to 48"

Figure 8.3 Doors, Residence: The primary entry of a house, often called the "front door," is nearly always 36 inches wide, 80 inches tall, 1-3/4 inches thick, solid core, and swings into the house. If the door uses two leaves, one will nearly always be fixed and act as a jamb for the other. While the leaves may seem indistinguishable from each other, subtle clues can be used to identify the moving leaf, which is the easiest to force entry.

a latch and a dead bolt. Unlike business entrance doors, these swing into the building, usually to a foyer, entry-way or living room.[7] If the house is two-story, the stairway to the upper floor is nearby (usually terminating at the front door) to allow escape in case of a fire. When there is a screen door, it will swing out.[8] These rules are so rigidly followed that they provide a useful diagramming principle called the Exterior Residential Door Rule, which states that *all residential entry doors swing into the building and are not less than 36 inches wide or more than 48 inches on any one leaf.*

When side-by-side doors are installed, only one leaf swings. The other leaf is called the "fixed" leaf. Anchored to the threshold and head (upper) jamb with throw-bolts, it acts as a jamb for the moving leaf. When necessary, it can be opened by opening the swinging leaf and then releasing the throw-bolts. Determining which one is

7. The age of the house is a good predictor for the type of room behind the entry door. On older houses, expect a living room; on newer houses expect a foyer or entryway.
8. This includes barred doors, sometimes called "burglar doors" or "narco doors."

the swinging leaf can be difficult since it is appears nearly identical to the fixed leaf. Determining the swinging leaf is critical for forced entries, however, because of the difficulty in forcing open the fixed leaf. A close examination will reveal several clues. For example, if there is a mail slot, it is almost always in the fixed leaf. The swinging leaf will have the dead-bolt and the peep hole. Potted plants or other porch ornamentation are never in front of the swinging leaf, but the doormat always is.

All buildings require more than one exit door, and houses are no exception. Furthermore, the doors must be far enough apart from one another so that one fire cannot simultaneously block both doors. Depending on the age of the house, they usually take on one of two forms. Older houses will have a swinging door of the same height as the front door (80 inches[9]) but only about 32 inches wide. These will also swing into the building, usually to a back porch, laundry room or kitchen area. If the house is of new construction the rear door is most often a sliding glass or French door[10] that opens into a family or living room from a patio.

Interior Doors

Businesses—Because the size, style and operation of doors for businesses are largely dependent on what the building is used for, they can vary widely. They also differ from interior residential doors in two ways. First, because they are used more frequently and often with less care, they are usually of more rugged construction. Second, they are commonly marked with signs that identify what is behind them. While this information is not easily obtained from outside the structure, virtu-

---

9. 80 inches is the most common height for doors of all kinds and uses.
10. French doors are hinged double doors that use a border of wood, resin or decorative metal around glass panes. They will swing into the building.

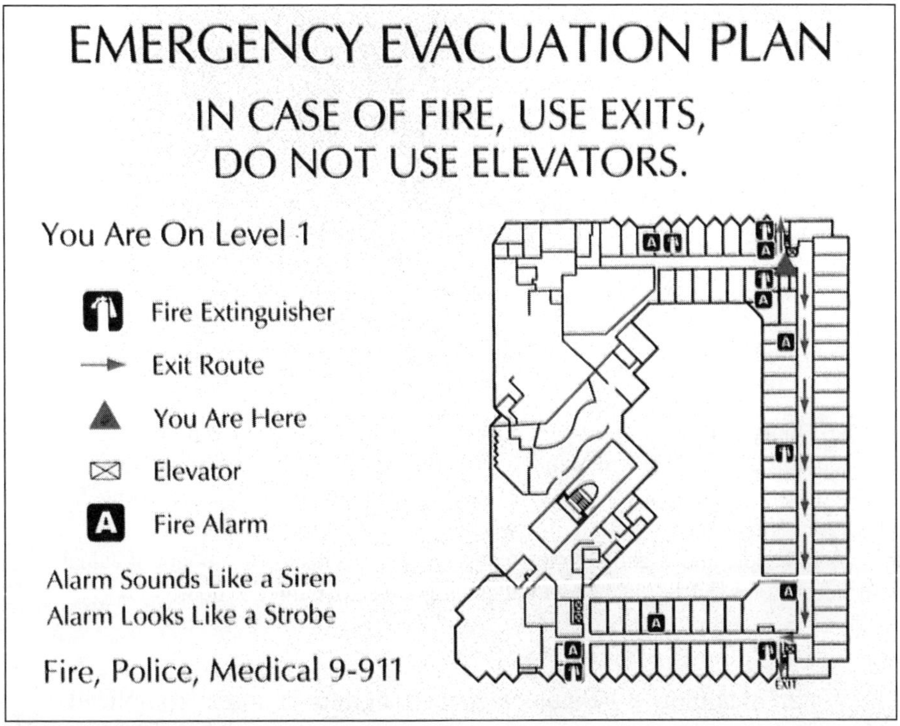

EMERGENCY EVACUATION PLAN

**IN CASE OF FIRE, USE EXITS,
DO NOT USE ELEVATORS.**

You Are On Level 1

- Fire Extinguisher
- Exit Route
- You Are Here
- Elevator
- Fire Alarm

Alarm Sounds Like a Siren
Alarm Looks Like a Strobe

Fire, Police, Medical 9-911

Figure 8.4 Exit Diagram: For buildings with high occupancy loads, many codes require fire escape plans to be publicly and conspicuously posted. Others require a current set of blueprints to be on file with the planning, zoning or building departments. The value of these for tactical diagramming can hardly be overestimated.

ally all businesses and public buildings are periodically subject to some type of inspection. Thus, access to the interior is not as difficult as for private residences, and critical tactical diagramming information can be obtained by using a ruse such as a burglary prevention check, fire prevention inspection or code compliance. Even better is that many municipalities require that a current set of blueprints be kept on file for some types of businesses. Consequently, a telephone call to the local building department or planning department may yield a bonanza of tactical diagramming information.

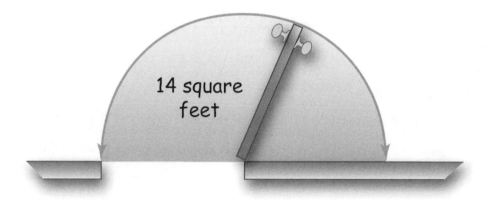

Figure 8.5 Door, Centered: A 36-inch door that swings 180 degrees requires nearly 14 square feet of floor space to be fully functional—as much as 10 percent of the floor space for an average-sized bedroom. This has resulted in a building practice of swinging doors into the room and against a wall. Light switches are nearly always mounted on the wall near the door handle and slightly higher. Consequently, a substantial amount of valuable tactical information can be gleaned with a quick glance at an interior door.

When obtaining a reliable tactical diagram is more complicated, there are still many useful indicators available. For example, in any building where the occupant load exceeds 100 people, signs are required for every door that is part of the exit system. Further, these signs must be illuminated.[11] In many buildings, such as large office buildings, apartments, hotels and the like, fire escape plans must be conspicuously posted. These are usually near the escalators, elevators or fire stairs and furnish a rudimentary floor plan that can be invaluable for tactical diagramming.

As stated earlier, doors are one of only two components in a structure that have to move to function. This fact becomes a very useful tool with swinging doors because the space necessary to swing them open must be unobstructed. For example, a 36-inch door swinging fully open to 180 degrees requires more than 14 square feet of floor space. This

---

11.   Most building codes will require illuminated exit signs with letters at least 6 inches tall and 3/4 inch wide.

represents a substantial loss of floor and wall space, especially when the door is fully functional when opened to only about 90 degrees. This has resulted in a building practice of placing doors in the corners of rooms and swinging them into the room and against a wall. Even though not required by any building code, this practice is so economical and efficient that it is almost universally applied.[12] Because hinged doors are the most common, this building practice yields another rule of thumb for tactical diagramming called the Interior Door Rule, which states that *generally, all interior doors swing into the room and against a wall.*[13]

Residences—A typical three-bedroom house has between seven and eleven interior doors servicing bedrooms, bathrooms and closets. It is uncommon to have doors servicing rooms such as family rooms and dining rooms because there is no need for privacy. Swinging doors are still the most common, but pocket doors[14] are also popular because they use no floor space. Other, less common types such as folding and sliding doors are used almost exclusively for closets. Like all doors, those servicing rooms inside residences are usually about 80 inches tall. However, they are only 1-3/8 inches thick and vary in width between 28 and 32 inches.[15]

Another interesting aspect of interior doors in residences is that the type of lock installed can be highly predictable. Generally these are either **passage locks** or **privacy locks**. The only difference between the two is that privacy locks can be locked and require a key[16] to open them. Passage locks are latches that hold the door shut when closed and

---

12. Because many building codes will not allow a door to cover a light switch when opened, another building practice is to place the light switch on the doorknob side of the door or, on rare occasions, on the wall that the door swings against but beyond the reach of the leaf.
13. This rule holds true for both business and residential doors.
14. Pocket doors are those that slide into a wall.
15. Doors that service closets are an exception and can easily be 8 feet long or longer. Furthermore, it is not uncommon to find floor-to-ceiling closet doors, especially in newer and luxury homes, to allow access to the entire closet. Nevertheless, these doors are so distinctive and have so little diagramming value that they are not discussed further here.
16. This is not a key in the conventional sense, but rather a notch, slot or hole to allow a screwdriver, coin or pin to unlatch the door.

can be opened simply by turning or depressing a knob. Because of the added expense of the more complex privacy locks, they are normally reserved for bathrooms, the master bedroom and on rarer occasions a den or home office.

When diagramming doors in a residence, keep in mind that interior doors will nearly always swing into a room and against a wall. This is true for even small rooms but will not include closets. With the single exception of walk-in closets and wardrobes, closet doors will swing away from the storage and into the room. On rare occasions, a bathroom door will swing out from the bathroom because there is no room to swing it in or to provide more privacy for a toilet.

Many building codes also require that a swinging door must not cover a light switch. Consequently, light switches can almost always be found on the inside wall of the room, slightly above the doorknob.[17] When for some reason a light switch can't be installed at this position, the next most common, albeit infrequent, location is at the same height on the adjacent wall beyond the width of the door.

Garage Doors

In rural areas and older areas of cities, detached garages are quite common. More modern tastes prefer attached garages on contemporary houses in both rural and urban settings. Regardless of which type is identified, garages are probably the easiest structure to diagram by understanding only a few building conventions.

Garages are fitted with two types of doors. The first type is for vehicles and is the one most often associated with garages, so much so that it is generically called a **"garage door."** Garage doors for single-vehicle entrances are generally 7 feet high and 9 feet wide. Garage doors for two vehicles are 7 feet high and 16 feet wide. Garage doors are overhead

---

17. Interior door hardware is typically set at 36 inches above the floor and light switches at 42 inches.

doors, swinging up toward the top of the door when opened.[18] They are nearly always either a single-piece **slab door**, which lifts up on hinges and is supported by heavy springs, or the more modern **sectional door** that rolls up on an overhead track. Both versions are frequently connected to an electric garage door opener and should always be assumed to be locked when in the closed position.

The second type of door found in garages is called a **pedestrian door**. This door is for people and follows all the conventions of the doors in the house. When located in a detached garage, these doors are usually located on a wall immediately adjacent to the vehicle door but can occasionally be found at the rear of the structure. Most pedestrian doors in a garage swing into the garage, but for security purposes, some are intentionally installed to swing out so that forcing them is more difficult.[19] Doors that swing out can be identified because the hinges can be seen; when the door swings away from you, the hinges will be on the other side of the door. Whenever a garage is attached, there will be a door connecting the garage with the house. This door typically enters into a kitchen or hallway and swings away from the living area and into the garage.[20] The most common attached garage is for two vehicles and has only one pedestrian door. If there is another, it typically exits to the outside along one of the sides of the garage.

For diagramming purposes, the identification of a garage is nearly diagnostic for determining floor plans. This is for two reasons. First, there are almost never interior walls of any sort. Garages are built to store vehicles and interior walls are a hindrance. Second, garages come

---

18. Some overhead garage doors, especially on garages constructed before 1950, are only 6-1/2 feet high. These are nearly always detached single-car garages. In rare instances, these garages use a sliding door on a trolley or a folding door, but the width remains about 9 feet.
19. Forcing a door open against the jamb requires between 30 and 50 times more energy than against the latch. Because modern jambs are often routed from a single piece of lumber, the door will often fail before the jamb.
20. While this door is usually the same height and width as other interior doors, it is typically 1-3/4 inches thick and "solid-core" to provide a fire barrier.

in standard sizes. Single-car garages are nearly always detached structures, 12–14 feet wide and 22–24 feet deep. Two-car garages may be detached or attached and are typically 22–24 feet in either direction. Some more modern houses, especially higher-priced ones, use a three-car garage. They are always attached to the dwelling and have one two-car door and one one-car door. Furthermore, they almost always have two pedestrian doors, one to the inside of the house and one that exits to the outside. Because the vehicle doors of a garage are among the easiest features of a structure to identify and locate, coupled with the standard widths, the size of the garage can be reliably estimated using the doors for the width and the standard depth of 22–24 feet.

One important note in diagramming garages is that many rural residences use a detached garage set back from the house. This style is not as prevalent as it once was and in urban locations is only found in older areas of the city. Detached garages, especially in urban areas, are often converted to dwellings. Depending on the climate, these conversions can usually be determined by looking for architectural features that seem out of place. For example, the presence of vents in the roof, especially combustion vents, is a good indicator, since except for a gas water heater, garages are seldom equipped with such appliances. The presence of windows is another hint. While some garages have windows in the walls, especially in rural areas, they are seldom found in urban settings and are almost never equipped with curtains or other coverings. When diagramming, none of these features by themselves should be considered conclusive but should not be cause for closer examination. As always, as the number of details you use to predict the location of inside features increases, so too does the degree of reliability and precision of your diagram.

CHAPTER 9

Windows

This is the longest chapter in the book, because more than any other architectural feature, windows have proven most useful for tactical diagramming. Not only their transparency but also their size, relationship to architectural features and each other, the curtains that cover them, and even the items stored or displayed on their sills[1] all provide clues to the rooms behind them. Almost all open in one or more directions and are a common point of entry for burglars and tactical teams, second only to doors. If, as the poets say, "the eyes are the windows of the soul," then windows are the eyes of a house. In fact, the word window comes from an old Norse word that meant "wind-eye." Windows were originally placed in structures solely for light and ventilation, but they also serve as fire escapes, so they are regulated by building and fire codes. These regulations, coupled with standard building practices, make windows among the most reliable of all a building's architectural features for determining floor plans.

Looking Through Windows

Before moving on to more complex methods of using windows to determine interior floor plans, let's elaborate on the obvious. Windows are

---

1. A window "sill" refers to the horizontal member that bears the upright portion of a frame or, more simply, the bottom of the window.

designed to look out of; consequently, we can look into them. Although this goes without saying, there are some techniques that can optimize the information obtained by looking through, and at, windows.

First, all glass reflects light—even clear glass. This means that you can only see through glass when the light is nearly equal, or stronger, on the opposite side. If you try and look through glass when the light is brighter on your side, all you'll see is a reflection. This phenomenon is especially noticeable with tinted glass and glass with plastic or metallic tinting applied. Because tinting is becoming increasingly popular as an energy conservation technique, some windows in houses and storefronts are impossible to see through without interior lighting.[2] Consequently

Figure 9.1 Window, Look Through: Besides the more subtle clues provided by a window's size, shape and location, much tactical diagramming information can be gained by simply looking through them. The best time for this is in the early evening hours when the occupants turn on lights but before they close the curtains.

2. In the United States, tinting is usually found on the southern and western exposures because these sides get the most sun. Window tinting is almost never used on the northern exposures for any building because this side is always in shadow.

the best time to see through dwelling windows is at dusk because the light is brighter inside when the occupants turn on their lights but it is early enough for them not to have pulled their window coverings.

Second, all windows are not created equal. Modern windows can be glazed with tempered glass, louvered glass, safety glass, tinted glass, even plastics that appear to be glass. The type of glass in a window can be used as an indicator for the type of room it serves. For instance, many, if not most, contemporary bathrooms use obscured glass to allow in light while retaining privacy. There is no other room in a house where such a high degree of privacy is desired, and accordingly, obscured glass is nearly diagnostic of a bathroom.[3] Steam on a window is another method of identifying a bathroom. In the same manner, the so-called "greenhouse windows"[4] are usually installed in kitchens.

Third, window coverings and items stored or displayed on the sill of a window provide strong clues to the nature and use of the rooms in which they are installed. Window coverings tend to be more formal in living and sleeping areas and less formal in bathrooms and food preparation areas. Lacy curtains do not hold up well in small, steamy bathrooms after a hot shower. In fact, most modern bathrooms don't use curtains at all. Pull-down blinds are often used to cover bedroom windows but almost never anywhere else. Venetian blinds and drapes are often used in both sleeping and living rooms. Just as important as window coverings are what is on the windowsill. Sports trophies and equipment or adolescent posters, for example, often indicate a child's room. Air freshener, soap or bubble bath bottles are strong clues for a bathroom.

Fourth, the lights shining through a window can be used as an indicator to identify rooms in a house or apartment. We have often heard it said that people are creatures of habit. Throughout our lives, there is

---

3. This is called the Obscured Glass Rule: *When a window has obscured glass; suspect a bathroom.*
4. Greenhouse windows are "bump out" windows, with shelves to provide light and space for small potted plants. They have been in vogue for only about 30 years or so, but are frequently installed on older houses and apartments, most commonly over the kitchen sink.

little of our behavior as ritualistic as getting ready to sleep. For example, as people prepare for sleep, the last light off in the house is usually the master bedroom; the second-to-last light is usually the bathroom that serves the master bedroom. The lights in children's bedrooms may precede these. Children's rooms may also have night lights. The light that stays on the longest in the evening is apt to be in the family or living room. When time and surveillance permit, much tactical intelligence can be gleaned by simply noting which lights come on, when, and for how long— and conversely, which lights are extinguished, when, and in what order.

An important thing to remember is to look at the window as well as through it. It would be wonderful to gain all the tactical intelligence we needed by a serendipitous peek through a window, but that is too much to hope for. Consequently, we need to use all of the information available to reliably predict a floor plan. The remainder of this chapter will describe more complex but reliable indicators that windows provide for tactical diagramming.

Size and Shape

The size and shape of a window provide strong clues as to the type of room behind it. Windows are hung from the top down, in a line with the top of a door, at 80 inches above the floor. Besides being more aesthetically pleasing, this practice allows the mass production of standard-sized curtains and drapes, which are much cheaper than custom window treatments. This practice is universal for dwellings and nearly universal for other types of buildings. Consequently, smaller windows with higher sills are used when furniture, beds or counters would otherwise obstruct the window. As a result, the size of a window and the height of the sill provide good indicators of what is behind them. Generally, the smallest windows are in bathrooms, the largest are living areas and the medium-sized ones are in sleeping and food preparation areas.

Small Windows—The smallest windows in a house are nearly

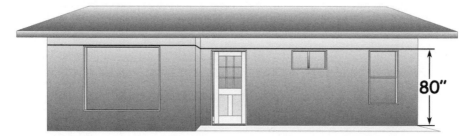

Figure 9.2 Window Alignment: Regardless of their style or shape, windows are hung from the top down (at the height of a door) instead of from the bottom up. Consequently, the height of the sills above the floor provide clues as to the type of room behind them.

always bathroom windows, which tend to be one of two shapes. On older houses they are long and narrow with a high sill and usually a double-hung or casement style. The double-hung style has two sliding components (called sashes) that can be slid up or down to allow ventilation (see Figure 9.3). A variation of the double-hung window is a single-hung where the top sash is fixed. These older double- and single-hung windows do not usually use obscured glass and often have curtains, albeit of vinyl or similar waterproof material.[5] The other common window in older houses is a casement window. A casement window has a hinge on one side and swings out. This type of window is popular in tropical areas of the country because it provides excellent ventilation when opened against a prevailing breeze. A variation of the casement window is called the louver window. A louver window has a series of horizontal slats that swing out to allow ventilation but do not let in rain. Both the casement and the louver windows were popular on homes and apartments constructed prior to the 1950s but are seldom seen on more contemporary structures as air conditioning became more economical and efficient.

---

5. While these curtains are usually waterproof, they are virtually indistinguishable at a distance from cloth and lace curtains. Consequently, they are extremely difficult to use in identifying a bathroom.

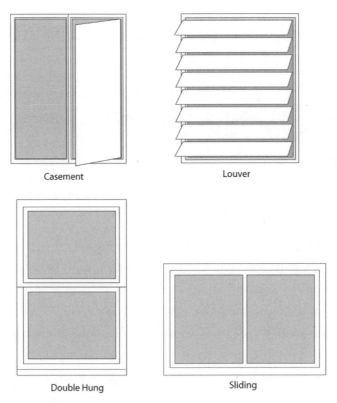

Casement

Louver

Double Hung

Sliding

Figure 9.3 Window Styles: While there are many styles of windows, four predominate for those installed in residences. The style of window provides clues to the age of the house and the type of room in which they are installed.

The second shape is very wide and short and almost always located high in the wall near the eaves. This is a more modern style and is most commonly a sliding window. Sliding windows are similar to the double-hung window except that the sash slides horizontally instead of vertically. These small windows seldom have muntins[6] but are routinely glazed with obscured or "clouded" glass.

By code, bathrooms must have windows of at least 3 square feet, one-

---

6. A muntin is simply a strip of wood or metal separating panes of glass. In modern construction, muntins are often mimicked as a single component that is installed over a single, large pane of glass for aesthetic reasons and to facilitate cleaning and glass replacement.

half of which must be openable, or have an approved mechanical ventilation system. Since design is almost always cheaper than hardware, most builders use the window for ventilation. On older houses the window is most often above the sink or toilet. On newer houses the sliding window is near the eaves and over the shower. One of the most reliable indicators of a bathroom window is when the width of the window is two or more times the height. In contemporary houses and apartments the sliding window must be high enough in the wall to clear the shower stall but still fit under the eaves. This requires them to be wide and short. This shape is so distinctive that it makes a bathroom the easiest room in the house to identify.[7]

Medium-Sized Windows—Medium-sized windows usually indicate either a sleeping or food preparation area. The key to telling the difference is the height of the sill and the area of the house. The windows in a kitchen need about 42 inches under them to clear the counters and backsplash, while bedroom windows usually need only about 36 inches. Thus, a window with a high sill is more likely to be a kitchen window than a bedroom window. If a window is identified in a kitchen, it is almost certainly over the sink. Look for other features to increase the reliability of your conclusion such as the water appliance vent above the window for the sink drain or the water heater combustion vent within 25 feet.[8]

Another factor in determining the difference between kitchen and bedroom windows is the area of the house in which they are located. First, bedrooms are not usually separated; that is, all the bedrooms are located in the same general area of the house. By identifying one bedroom you can anticipate another close by. As a result, we can reasonably expect to find a greater number of medium-sized windows grouped together at one end of a house or apartment.

---

7. This can be expressed as the W=2H Rule: *When the width of the window is twice or more the height, it is almost always a bathroom window.*
8. A very common building practice is to place a water heater within 25 feet of the kitchen sink (and often closer) because of the high demand for hot water for washing and cooking.

The age of the house provides a very dependable clue to whether the area you are examining is a sleeping or a food preparation area. In older homes the bedrooms were most often located at the rear of the house and the living areas in the front. Newer homes have the sleeping area at one end of the house, which may include the front, and the living area at the rear. The food preparation area is usually separated from the sleeping area.

Large Windows—The largest windows of the house are almost always in the living areas. In older houses they face the street, and in more modern houses they face into the backyard. Although double- and single-hung windows are common in older houses, new homes usually have fixed and/or sliding windows. A strong indicator that you are looking into a living area is a bay or bow window. These windows project out from the wall and provide three to six large panes (called lights) for each window. Besides providing light and ventilation, these windows provide space and often have window seats. These are also among the most expensive a builder can install in a house, often running to thousands of dollars. As a result, these windows are used sparingly and are a strong indicator that the room behind them is either a living room or the master bedroom. Larger and more luxurious homes may use them for dining rooms. They are virtually never seen in apartments, but some townhouses have scaled-down versions.

When examining surveillance photographs of large windows, use a strong, illuminated magnifying glass, since they are large enough to be able to see through. If the reflection is not excessive you may actually be able to see into the room behind.

Relationship

The relationship of windows to other windows and architectural features is among the most dependable of all clues for locating interior walls. This is because of several building practices.

Figure 9.4 Window Shape: Houses always have different sizes of windows. Their shape, size and relationship to each other provide strong clues as to what type of room they serve. The smallest windows are reserved for bathrooms, where privacy is the main concern. Medium-sized windows, especially with high sills (to allow a bed headboard under them), are for sleeping areas, and the largest windows are reserved for living areas. A small window between two medium-sized ones often indicates a bathroom between two bedrooms, especially if the shape of the window is two or more times its height, and obscured glass is nearly conclusive.

First, although not to the same degree as bathrooms, bedrooms are an area of the house where privacy is desired. This especially includes sound. It is a standard building practice to place closets and bathrooms between bedrooms to provide better sound insulation. Because of the size, shape and type of glass commonly found in bathroom windows, they are the easiest to identify in a structure. And, once located, they provide a strong clue that a bedroom is adjacent. A bathroom will often service two bedrooms, one on each side.

Second, other architectural features such as vents, doors, chimneys, skylights and other windows provide more precise and reliable clues together than alone. Use as many indicators as possible to strengthen your predictions. For example, two medium-sized windows separated by a small one is a strong indicator for a bathroom between two bedrooms. Likewise, a medium-sized window with a high sill and a water appliance vent on the roof nearby is a good indication of a kitchen window over a sink.

Third, many building codes require that all inhabitable rooms have windows of at least 10 square feet or 10 percent of the floor area, which-ever is greater. This is because of the potential need to use a window as a fire escape. Many local building codes require even more window area. As a result, the amount of window area can provide a clue to the size of the room behind. One exception to this rule is hotels and motels above the fourth floor line. This is for two reasons. First, floors above the fourth are excluded because that is as high as the ladders of most fire trucks can reach, and second, the code requires more fire-resistant construction above this floor.

Window Analysis

Among the most reliable and precise of all methods for determining interior walls is with a **window analysis**. It is a simple procedure yet yields a considerable amount of useful tactical diagramming information. It begins by understanding a building practice of installing windows in the middle of rooms. It is not required anywhere, but for aesthetic reasons we want our windows in the middle of rooms. This custom is nearly universal and yields the Window Analysis Rule: *The distance between*

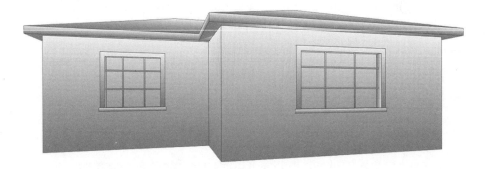

Figure 9.5 Window Analysis Example: A "window analysis" is possible because of the nearly universal building practice of locating windows in the center of room walls for aesthetic reasons. This technique is a powerful tool for tactical diagramming because of its ability to predict walls and rooms with no other visible architectural features, such as closets.

a known wall and a window is equal to the distance between a suspected wall and the window. That's it! That is all you have to remember.

Now here is how the analysis works. When you observe a window you can assume it is in the middle of the wall of an interior room. The distance between the window and a known wall (such as an exterior wall) is distance K, or the known distance. Use this measurement on the other side of the window to find P, or the predicted distance from the window to an anticipated interior wall.

Here are a few examples to demonstrate how easy it is to use. In Figure 9.6 we see the gable end of a house with one window. We measure the distance between the known (exterior) wall of the house and the window. This is K, our known distance. Since we know that the window is probably in the middle of the room we simply transfer the known distance, K, to the other side of the window. This provides us with a predicted distance, designated P. The interior wall can then be determined with a high degree of accuracy by using our two known distances—the exterior wall to the window (K) and the width of the window (W)—plus

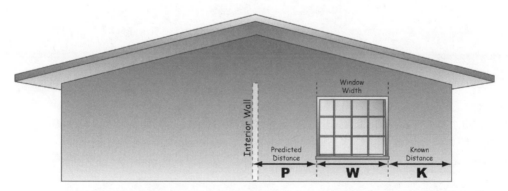

Figure 9.6 WA Basic: The window analysis formula is K+W+P=I. It works by first determining the known distance (K) from the edge of a window to a known wall (usually an exterior wall) and then measuring the same distance on the other side of the window. Then simply add the known distance to the width of the window and the predicted distance.

our predicted distance (P) to locate where an interior wall is likely to be. This is expressed in the formula K+W+P=I.

Those with construction experience will note that exterior walls and interior walls may vary in thickness by as much as several inches but the formula makes no allowance for this. This is because we are attempting to draw a diagram, not a set of blueprints. You are certainly free to allow for the width of the exterior wall (about 5 inches[9]) but for most applications that is more precision than is necessary. In fact, it is more precise than may be possible since most diagramming techniques don't provide the degree of precision that a window analysis does. You will be doing exceptionally well if you can predict the location of an interior wall to within a foot or so.

Let's do a few more examples. In Figure 9.7 we see the gable end of another house, this time with two windows. We determine our known

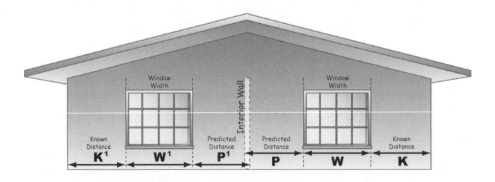

Figure 9.7 WA Two Windows: In this example, the known distances (K and K1) are easily determined, as are the window widths (W and W1). Because the predicted distances (P and P1) coincide, the probability of an interior wall is even more certain.

---

9. The width of an exterior wall will vary with the type of construction. For most wood frame houses, allow approximately 5 inches. In colder climates, 2x6s are often used as studs to allow for more insulation and the wall will be about 8 inches. Masonry walls are considerably thicker and can be as wide as 12 inches. Most, however, are about 8 inches, excluding inside wall coverings such as drywall.

distances (K and K1)[10] and use them to determine our predicted distances (P and P1). We note that they coincide very closely. Thus we can predict to an even higher certainty than in the first example that there is an interior wall located where the P distances join. This emphasizes the Cardinal Rule of Diagramming[11] and serves to encourage us to use as many features as possible to increase our precision and reliability. This could be several windows, a window and a vent, or any combination.

One of the most beneficial uses for a window analysis is predicting rooms and walls where no outside features exist. For instance, look at the house depicted in Figure 9.8. We see the gable end of a house with two windows. We determine our known distances and use them to determine our predicted distances. This time, however, there is an unexplained gap between the P distances. We determine this gap to be about 3 feet. Since we know that it is customary to place closets

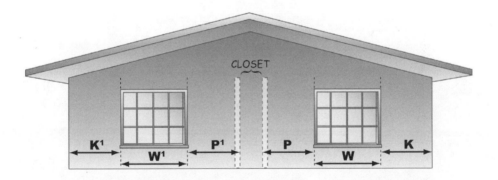

Figure 9.8 WA Closet: In this illustration, the K+W+P=I formula reveals an unaccountable space. Because closets are often used as sound barriers between bedrooms and the width between the suspected walls is of approximately the right width (about 30–36 inches), we suspect a closet.

---

10. Note: While the K and K1 distances (or P and P1) may be the same, never assume it! They will be different in rooms of different sizes. When using more than one window, always measure the distances and identify them as distinct to avoid confusion, especially with large buildings.

11. As the number of details you use to predict the location of inside features increases, so does the degree of reliability and precision of your diagram.

between bedrooms for soundproofing we can then predict that each of our P distances is pointing to a separate interior wall. The advantage of using this method for determining the location of these otherwise "invisible" rooms is difficult to exaggerate. There is no other method that is as likely to determine the location of closets since there are no outside architectural features which distinguish them.

For our next example look at the house in Figure 9.9. This depicts the side of a house with three windows. One smaller window is between two larger ones. We obtain our known distances by examining the spaces between each exterior wall and the adjacent windows (K and K1). Using these known distances we can then determine our predicted distances. But once again we have a large gap between our predicted distances. This time, however, we see a window in the gap. Because we know that the window is most likely in the middle of a room, and because we can predict where the interior walls are likely to be, we can use the distance

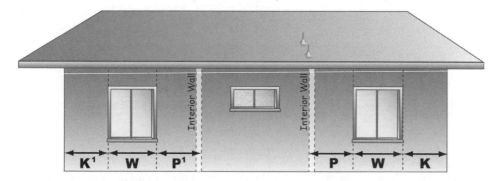

Figure 9.9 WA Basic: We can continue to use the window analysis formula by measuring the distances between the window in the gap and our suspected interior walls. We note that the distances (P2) are not only equal but also coincide with those predicted by the initial assessment. Further, we see two water appliance vents directly in line with the suspected wall on the right. The number of features used tremendously increase the reliability of our prediction that the interior walls are indeed there. Further, because the water appliance vents proceed directly upward through the wall we can be certain there is no door in the wall underneath them.

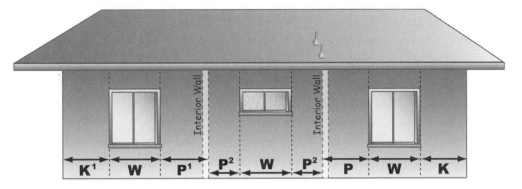

Figure 9.9a WA Complex: After conducting our initial assessment using the window analysis formula, we note that the predicted interior walls are quite far apart. This time, however, we also see a window in the center of the gap. Because it is twice as wide as it is high, we suspect a bathroom.

between this window and the probable location of an interior wall. We designate this distance as P2, because it is still a predicted distance. No matter how strongly we believe the wall is likely to be there, it is still a prediction, not a certainty. Therefore we designate the distance as a prediction (P) not a known (K).

Once we have determined that the predicted (P) measurements on each side of the middle window are equal and that each indicates the likelihood of an interior wall we already suspected (because of our measurements with the other two windows using known distances) we can achieve a higher degree of reliability and precision.

Spot Check

Using the same house, let's examine it just a little bit more. Using a photograph, there would be a number of outside architectural features that we could examine to make our predictions, but this sketch has intentionally eliminated all the architectural details except the roof, windows, vents and exterior walls. But even with this limited information, see how much we can reliably estimate about the interior.

First, we know that there are at least three rooms on this side of the house. Second, the larger windows are most likely bedrooms and the center one is a bathroom. Why? Because, like closets, bathrooms are also used between bedrooms for sound insulation. You can guess that it is a bathroom because you see that the window is glazed with obscured glass and that it is two or more times wider than it is high. The window coupled with your recognition of the water appliance vents is an extremely strong indicator of a bathroom.

Third, the water appliance vents are near the eave and over an interior wall. That they are located so near the eaves is a strong indicator that they are exactly above the interior wall in which they are installed.

Fourth, the fact that there are two vents very close together indicates the lack of a stack vent system; therefore each vent services a different water appliance. While you can attribute one to the bathtub/shower under the narrow bathroom window with the high sill, the other must be for either the sink or toilet along the same wall. And, because the vents extend into a wall that separates a bedroom, it is unlikely that there is an interior door in that wall because it is hard to route pipes around an opening as big as a door (not to mention the appliances themselves).

Figure 9.10 Spot Check: By using even a few tactical diagramming techniques, we gain an ability to "see" inside a house. In this illustration we see the same house we've been diagramming as if the walls were translucent, because we've been able to determine the location of walls, types of rooms, and even the probable location of the tub and shower in the bathroom. Even when we can't determine what is there, we can eliminate what can't be there, such as the lack of a door in the wall under the water appliance vents.

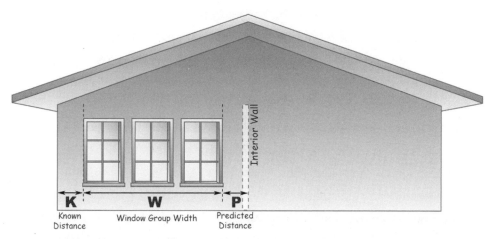

Figure 9.11 Window Groups: Occasionally, a series of tall but narrow windows will be "grouped." To determine if windows are grouped, one good rule of thumb is whenever the distance between the windows is less than the known distance (K), then consider the windows as a single component.

This would require that the bathroom door be in the wall separating the left bedroom or in the interior wall near the center of the house, most likely exiting into a hallway. Hence, if you had to choose, your best guess would be that the bedroom on the left might be the master bedroom since it would be most common to enter the master bath directly from the master bedroom.

Fifth, if you had already determined that the master bedroom was somewhere else or that the door to this bathroom was in the interior wall closest to the center of the house, it would contra-indicate the master bedroom and encourage you to look for additional clues.

Window Groups

Before completing our examination of windows it is necessary to clarify one potential misinterpretation. Occasionally you may run across two or more windows that are located very close to each other. This configuration is often used when large areas of a wall are used for windows. The spaces between the windows hide posts that support a header over the windows. The header and posts are used to transfer the weight of the ceiling, upper floor and roof around the windows to the foundation. With one adjustment, the window analysis formula remains the same. The adjustment simply treats the group of windows as a single component.

To determine whether or not you need to use the adjustment, note the size and type of the windows and the space between them. The strongest indicator is the space. If the space between each of the windows is less than the known distance (K), then treat the windows as one component. Use the known distance to predict the location of the interior wall by placing it completely on the other side of the group of windows. The window analysis technique works the same by simply treating all the windows in the group as a single window. One additional caveat, however, is that this configuration is often used in the corners of large rooms (usually living areas) rather than in the middle.

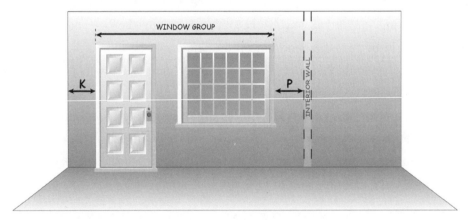

Figure 9-12 Door Window: One common configuration for windows, especially with motels and apartments, is when the main door is immediately adjacent to a large window. When the door swings toward the window both the door and the window are in the same room (nearly always the living room). To diagram this configuration simply treat the door and the window as a window group and measure the known distance (K) from the side of the door and use the measurement to get the predicted distance (P) on the other side of the window.

The examples we've used to demonstrate the window analysis technique are void of all but the rudimentary architectural details necessary to make a point. Surveillance photographs are rich with clues providing insight into the interior floor plan. The key to successful tactical diagramming is using the information you have in a new way.

CHAPTER 10

Rooms

It goes without saying that all buildings are comprised of one or more rooms, and understanding the nature of those rooms can provide a wealth of insight into tactical diagramming. For instance, almost without exception, rooms are rectangular. Consequently, the floor plan of a house or apartment can be determined by arranging a series of rectangles to match the visible architectural features according to standard building practices and rules. Furthermore, if you can determine the length of any two adjacent walls, the entire rectangle can be reliably calculated, since the opposing walls must be of the same length. This is stated as the Rectangle Rule: *Because houses are constructed from a series of rectangular rooms, determining the length of any two adjacent walls in a room provides a reliable method for calculating the remaining two since the opposing walls must be the same. By repeating this method with other rooms, the entire shape of the house is revealed.*

Rooms also tend to be somewhat similar to their counterparts in other houses. Kitchens will always have a stove, sink, refrigerator and cupboards. Bathrooms will always have a toilet and sink, and most times a shower and/or tub. In addition, rooms tend to be arranged in somewhat predictable patterns. The dining room is next to the kitchen. Bedrooms tend to be located next to one another. Bathrooms and closets are placed between bedrooms for soundproofing. Rooms also tend to be standard in size. The smallest rooms in the house are the bathrooms, followed by the kitchen. The largest is almost always a family room, followed by the living room. The master bedroom is always larger than the other bedrooms. Because of all these similarities, we have a considerable amount of useful information for tactical diagramming without ever having seen

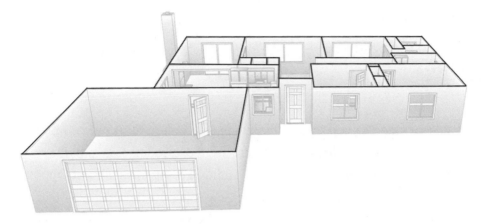

Figure 10.1 House, Rectangles: Because the rooms in a house are nearly always in the form of a rectangle, determining the lengths of any two adjacent sides provides the shape of the rectangle since the opposing sides must be mirror opposites. By arranging these rectangles according to architectural features, such as vents, windows and doors, the shapes and sizes of the both the individual rooms and the house as a whole become evident.

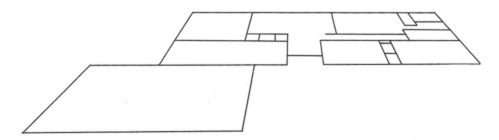

Figure 10.1a House, Rectangles: A sketch of the same house (in perspective) might appear like this. This is assuming far more detail than can usually be gained from architectural features alone, however, and tactical diagrams are never drawn in perspective. They usually take the form of a pencil sketch in a notebook or on graph paper.

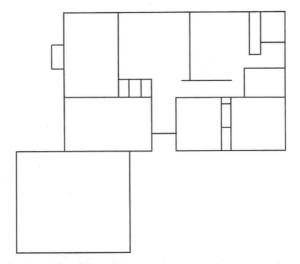

Figure 10.1b House, Rectangles: The rectangle method provides a quick and easy method of obtaining the approximate shapes and sizes of the rooms and the house. Even without additional information, such as windows and doors, nearly any tactical team would be ecstatic to receive just the information as sketched above.

the building. This yields another tactical diagramming principle called the Intuitive Rule. Simply put, this rule states, *When in doubt, use your own home for insight.* This is because there will be more similarities than differences between the house or apartment you live in and the one you are attempting to diagram.

While this principle is very practical as is, we can make it even more useful by providing additional information on particular rooms.

Kitchens

Every house has one kitchen and only one. Kitchens are important in tactical diagramming because they are second only to bathrooms as the most common place to destroy perishable evidence such as illegal drugs. Kitchens are work spaces, and in older construction a kitchen was often separated from the rest of the house by doors so that the other occupants wouldn't be disturbed while food was being prepared.

In more modern construction, kitchens may adjoin breakfast nooks, dining rooms or family rooms without doors, and in many cases without even walls. These open floor plans treat kitchens as an extension of the dining space, and building codes refer to the entire area simply as a "food preparation area."

Building codes normally require kitchens to be a minimum of 50 square feet, but they are typically about twice that size and in large, older houses can easily reach 150 square feet. Kitchens are built to maximize the use of three appliances. These are the refrigerator, stove and sink. In between these appliances are cupboards and counter space. The "paths" between these appliances are usually referred to as the **work triangle**, which is used as a measure of efficiency of the kitchen. If the total lengths of the legs of this triangle are less than about 12 feet, there is too little counter space, and if they are more than 22 feet[1] it is considered an inefficient layout. Furthermore, the kitchen sink is invariably under a window. As a result, kitchens are among the most predictable rooms to diagram and, almost without exception,[2] take on one of four configurations.[3]

The first configuration is the **U-shape**. This plan places each appliance on a separate wall and is considered one of the best designs because there is no "flow-through" foot traffic to interfere with the work. Because most of the work is done at the sink, every attempt is made to place it between the stove and refrigerator at the apex of the work triangle.

The second configuration is **L-shape**. This plan places two appliances on one wall and the other on an adjacent wall perpendicular to

1. Other figures given for an efficient work triangle vary from 11 to 26 feet.
2. The single exception is with older houses, in which the kitchen is built as a separate room. Even for these rooms, the floor plans typically follow one of the four configurations described.
3. Some books will describe six or more configurations by enclosing one end of the kitchen with a counter, peninsula or island. Most kitchen designers, however, consider these as simply adaptations of the four basic designs described here.

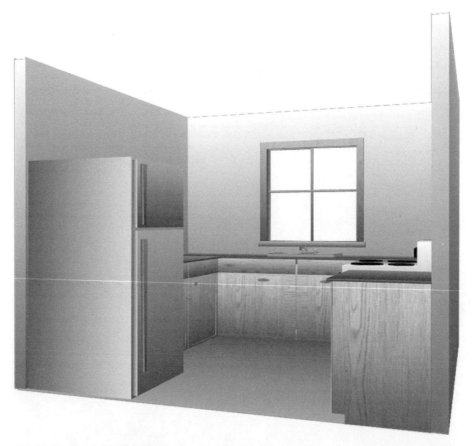

Figure 10.2 Kitchen, U-Shape: This U-shaped configuration is commonly used at one end of a house since there is no "flow through" to interrupt the food preparation and cleaning. (Upper cabinets intentionally omitted for clarity.)

the first. As before, the ideal is to place the sink in the middle, between the stove and refrigerator. This style is very popular because it can be installed in a corner of the building and a dining room table or breakfast nook can be placed in the open fourth corner.

The third configuration is the **galley**, sometimes called the **double-counter**. This plan installs the appliances and counters along two parallel walls, open at each end via either a door or a breakfast nook. Because this allows foot traffic through the work area, a minimum of 5 feet is

Figure 10.3 Kitchen, L-Shape: Like the other designs, the L-shaped kitchen floor plan is arranged to maximize use of the stove, sink and refrigerator. Another commonality between all kitchen floor plans is a window over the kitchen sink. (Upper cabinets intentionally omitted for clarity.)

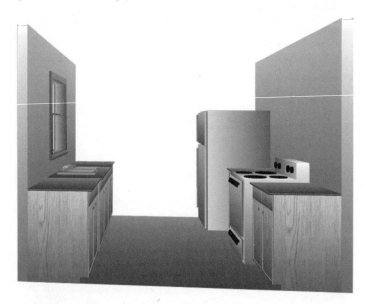

Figure 10.4 Kitchen, Galley: The galley design is also called a double-counter design. Because this design allows for "flow-through traffic," a minimum of 4 feet (5 feet is preferred) is needed between the counters. This design is popular because it allows for a lot of counter space. (Upper cabinets intentionally omitted for clarity.)

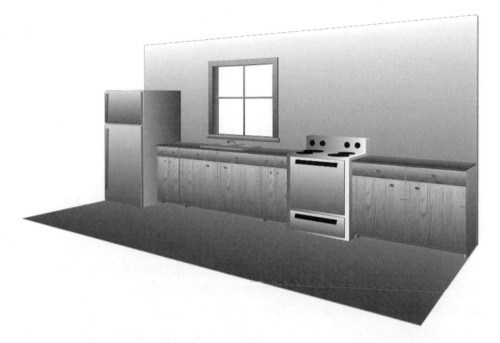

Figure 10.5 Kitchen, In-Line: Because they tend to be small, single-line floor plans for kitchens are popular in apartments. Because foot traffic is not normally a problem, only about 3 feet in front of the counters is necessary to allow full use of the three major appliances. In this configuration, the sink is always preferred to be the middle appliance. (Upper cabinets intentionally omitted for clarity.)

needed between the counters. Galley kitchens are popular because they have a lot of counter space.

The last configuration is the **single-line** or **in-line** plan. This plan places all the appliances and counters along a single wall. Kitchens using this plan tend to be very small and are popular in apartments. Because foot traffic is not usually a problem, there needs to be only 3 feet between the front of the counters and any other obstacle, such as a table or another wall.

Bathrooms

Bathrooms weren't always required in a house. In fact, the first wooden bathtubs, immortalized in the old western movies, didn't appear until about the mid 1800s, and bathrooms didn't come inside houses until the

1920s. They first arrived in the urban areas, largely as a result of health and privacy concerns, and were made possible by improved plumbing. Modern building codes now require each dwelling to have at least one toilet, sink, and either a bathtub or a shower, often configured as a combination bathtub/shower.

Bathrooms are typically the smallest rooms in a house[4] and vary from 5 by 7 feet to 5 by 11 feet.[5] In contemporary styles, a **half-bath** or "guest bath" is also popular and excludes the tub or shower. Guest baths can be as small as 3 by 6 feet. Bathrooms are also one of the most frequently used rooms in a house, usually shared by every resident.[6] Bathrooms use more plumbing than any other room in a house. Consequently, remodeling virtually never changes their floor plans because of the exorbitant costs of moving the drains and connections inside the walls and floors. Because of the deleterious effects of moisture generated in bathrooms, building codes require that they be equipped with a window of at least 3 square feet, half of which must be openable to vent the excess moisture. The only other alternative is a ventilator capable of changing the air in the room every 12 minutes. Because a window is usually less expensive and more durable than an electric ventilator, good bathroom designs nearly always include a window.[7] In older houses this is usually a double-hung window over the toilet or sink, but modern styles almost always use a sliding window over the tub. Because bathrooms require the highest degree of privacy in a home, the glass is almost always obscured and the doors are equipped with privacy locks.[8]

---

4. Bathrooms are so small that when remodeling an older house, large closets are sometimes converted to bathrooms.
5. While closets will be smaller, they are not usually considered rooms in the conventional sense of the word.
6. This excludes only the master bathroom that is popular in large, contemporary homes and typically used only by the owners or tenants.
7. Bathroom windows are usually the most distinctive of a given house and are virtually diagnostic. For more information on bathroom windows, see Chapter 9.
8. Privacy locks are designed for locking but do not normally require a key to unlock. For more information on doors and locks, see Chapter 8.

Like kitchens, bathrooms are built around three appliances.[9] These are the toilet, a sink, and a bathtub and/or shower.[10] One of the useful aspects of this for diagramming purposes is that while they may vary in shape, style and color to a great extent, they vary only slightly in size. This makes them highly predictable. Like military clothing, toilets and tubs are "size small—fits all." In fact, a short browse through a builder's catalog will tell you that tubs are about 5 feet long by 2-1/2 feet wide. Showers may be anywhere from 3 by 3 feet to 3 by 5 feet. Toilets are about 2 feet 4 inches long by about 1 foot 8 inches wide. Furthermore, toilets and counters need at least 18 inches clearance in front, and tubs and showers need between 18 and 24 inches of clearance for comfortable use.[11] For diagramming purposes, sinks are nearly irrelevant because they are set into countertops that may vary from 3 feet to more than 8 feet.[12] In fact, modern styles quite commonly install more than one sink in a single countertop in a "his and hers" style.[13]

When diagramming bathrooms, use these tips:

- Bathrooms are frequently located between bedrooms for easy access and as additional soundproofing.
- Because of the frequent need for fresh towels, washcloths and the like, it is very common to locate a linen closet in close proximity.
- Tubs and showers tend to occupy an entire wall. That is, they take up one end of the entire room with nothing on either side.

---

9. Just as often referred to as "fixtures."
10. In luxurious houses, a bidet may also be installed. Notwithstanding, they are so rare and these houses are so seldom tactical targets that they are not worth describing here.
11. Bathroom designers often use a "turnaround circle" of 5 feet. This means that an ideal bathroom design should allow a circle of 5 feet in diameter between all the fixtures.
12. With extremely rare exceptions, however, countertops are always about 2 feet in depth.
13. In more luxurious homes, the sinks are often set in a "powder room," which is always immediately adjacent to the bathroom but more open with less privacy. There is usually only one of these rooms for each house and they are always near or part of the master bedroom/bathroom and often near a walk-in closet.

Figure 10.6 Bathroom, Corridor: One of the most common configurations for a bathroom, especially in older houses, is called the **corridor**. This floor plan places the three appliances—sink, toilet and bathtub—in a U-shaped design. A double-hung window is often over the toilet or sink, but never over the bathtub/shower. Interestingly, the window is seldom glazed with obscured glass. (Front wall and shower sides removed for clarity.)

- Two very common configurations for family bathrooms are the **corridor**, with a tub/shower combination on one side and the sink and toilet on the other, and the in-line plan, which allows all the plumbing to be installed in a single wall.

    Because of the small room size, bathroom doors are difficult to install. Consequently, the wall against which they swing[14] is nearly

---

14. Interior doors customarily swing into rooms and against walls. For more information on doors, see Chapter 8..

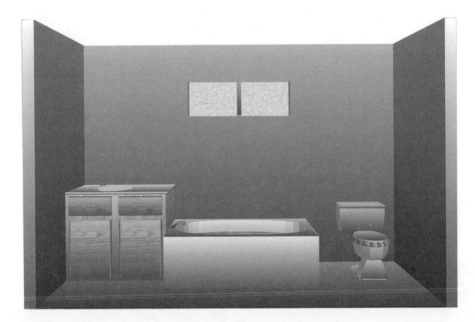

Figure 10.7 Bathroom, In-Line: The in-line floor plan takes advantage of a common wall to install all the plumbing. While both floor plans are often found in newer houses, this design is seldom found in older houses. One distinctive feature of this design is the window over the bathtub/shower. It is nearly always a sliding window, twice (or more) as long as it is high, and glazed with obscured glass. This design meets building code requirements for ventilation while still allowing privacy. It is so distinctive that, once recognized, it identifies not only the bathroom but also the shower inside. (Front wall and shower sides removed for clarity.)

always devoid of appliances or counters. Some contemporary designs may use a pocket door that slides into a wall.

Because the sizes and number of bathroom appliances are fixed, locating the window and door (and which way the door swings) may be all that is needed to diagram the rest of the room.

Bedrooms

Bedrooms are so critical to a residence that they are used as a means to categorize them. For instance, houses and apartments are usually advertised as "three-bedroom houses" and "two-bedroom apartments." More

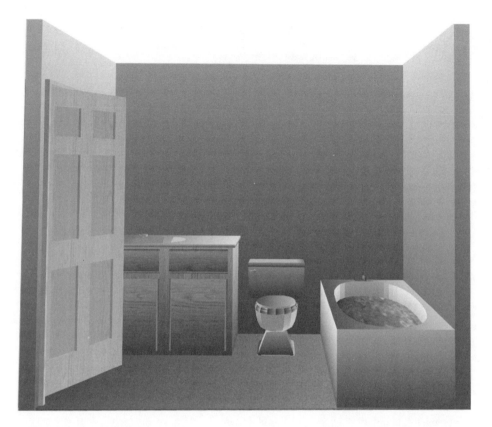

Figure 10.8 Bathroom, L-Shape: Like the in-line floor plan, the L-shape bathroom takes advantage of a single wall to house all the plumbing. Sometimes called the "wet wall," this wall is often constructed from 2 x 6-inch studs to allow room for the plumbing. In this configuration, the toilet is most often located behind the sink and counter for additional privacy. The door swings against the near wall (not shown for clarity). This configuration can be used in a space as small as 5 by 7 feet, making it about the size of a walk-in closet. (Near wall and shower sides removed for clarity.)

bedrooms are becoming the norm in modern design, and more than a third of all new housing in the last decade has included four bedrooms. The selling point is that if a family doesn't need the extra bedroom for one of their children, it can easily be converted into a home office, den or sewing room.

Generally, bedrooms come in two styles, master and everything else. The master bedroom is intended for the owner or tenant of the residence and is commensurately larger and more elegant than the others. Besides a bed and one or more chests of drawers, master bedrooms frequently include an entertainment center, chairs and a dresser or small table. Contemporary designs are nearly always served by a private bathroom accessed only through the master bedroom. In fact, master bedrooms in expensive houses can be very elaborate, equipped with a balcony and sliding door, fireplace, powder room, walk-in closet and a large master bath, complete with a Jacuzzi tub. Even in less expensive houses, however, master bedrooms are larger than the other bedrooms in the structure.

The second style of bedroom includes all the other bedrooms in the residence. In all but the most luxurious houses, these are used for children, and occasionally guests. They are smaller than the master bedroom and share a bath. In older houses the closets are usually equipped with a swinging door that swings out into the bedroom and against a wall. Contemporary designs have larger closets and are typically equipped with sliding doors. Regardless of the age of the house, the closets are almost always separating the bedroom from another bedroom or living space to provide soundproofing. Because all bedrooms are intended for sleeping comfort and privacy, they are most often located away from the noisier food preparation areas. When diagramming bedrooms, consider these design practices:

- To provide privacy and reduce noise, bedrooms are almost always located near one another at one end of a house. This is especially commonplace in two-story structures where all the bedrooms will be located on the second story and none on the first.[15]
- On both single- and two-story houses, bedrooms can usually be found at one end of the building and are almost never found near the food preparation area. Because two bedrooms with closets and/or a

---

15. This may not be the case if a house has been remodeled and existing bedrooms have remained downstairs.

bathroom between them occupy substantial space, they can often be found on both corners of one end of the building.

• Because bedrooms are second only to bathrooms in their need for privacy, the doors will usually open into a common hallway rather than directly into a living area.

• One of the easiest methods of identifying bedrooms is by noting the size and location of the windows. Because bathroom windows are the most conspicuous in a house, first locate a bathroom and then look for a medium-sized window with high sills adjacent. The sills are high to allow a bed with a headboard underneath.[16]

Living and Family Rooms

Living and family rooms are the most public in a residence. This is where visitors are greeted and guests are entertained. The more modern living room evolved from the older drawing room or parlor. These rooms were specifically designed to greet guests, and even today, living rooms tend to be the most formal in the house. Family rooms are a relatively recent convention and are where a family spends most of its time with activities like watching television, reading, studying or playing. Consequently, a family room is the most likely location for the family television and/or computer. It is also the busiest room in the house.

Older houses usually have the living room on the street side of the house. This practice is so common that in many areas of the country this room is still called the "front room." The living room in these houses does double duty because there is almost never a family room. In more modern construction, the living room tends to be away from the street and the family room is adjoining with a door that exits to

---

16. For fire escape reasons, building codes will require a bedroom window of at least 24 inches tall by 20 inches wide and with a sill not more than 44 inches above the floor. Most bedroom windows, however, are considerably larger than the requirements.

the patio and back yard. Because these rooms typically have no appliances[17] they are not constrained like bathrooms or kitchen. Likewise, they have no closets and do not conform to patterns and practices of sleeping areas. Compounding the problem even further, they may not even have common walls because they often open to other rooms such as the foyer, a dining room and each other. In fact, a popular contemporary design combines the living and family rooms into one large room called a "great room." Because of these reasons, these rooms may be odd-shaped and even have cathedral ceilings that will affect the floor plans of the second story. When diagramming family and living rooms, these tips will help:

- The largest windows in a house are usually in these rooms. Consequently, a look through them may yield a bounty of useful and otherwise unavailable tactical diagramming information. The best time to accomplish this is at dusk when the house begins to get dark and the occupants turn on the lights but have not yet drawn the curtains for the evening.
- Because of the popularity of computers and televisions, especially large-screen TVs, these are often visible through windows and will assist in identifying these rooms.
- Family rooms in contemporary houses are often located near the kitchen and have an exit door to a patio. Because patio covers are highly conspicuous from the air, the location of a family room may be approximated from an aerial photograph and confirmed by a process of elimination after the kitchen, bathrooms and bedrooms are identified by other, more reliable architectural features.
- Likewise, because fireplaces are popular in family rooms, locat-

---

17. One exception is that more modern construction may have a wet bar in a family room with a small sink.

ing a chimney, especially a masonry chimney with a downstairs fireplace,[18] is a good indicator of a family room.

- Regardless of the age of the house, living rooms always tend to be located in close proximity to the entrance door. In older houses and small apartments, the front door nearly always opens directly into the living room. In more modern construction it will open into a small foyer, which in turn is open to the living room.
- Because family rooms are the busiest in a house, they are frequently located next to the kitchen and away from bedrooms because of noise.[19]

Minor Rooms

Minor rooms, such as laundry rooms, pantries and walk-in closets, are function-specific, which is to say they are designed for one purpose and one purpose only. Until fairly recently, they were considered luxuries. With the exception of walk-in closets, they seldom exist in older homes and are found even more rarely in smaller apartments. Nowadays, however, any or all of these rooms may be found in even moderately priced contemporary houses. While they are seldom of critical tactical value, an ability to predict their location may assist in diagramming other rooms. For that reason, the following information is provided:

- Laundry rooms are nearly always located off the kitchen and near the garage. In fact, it is quite common to have a washer and dryer in

---

18. This can be determined when the width of the masonry chimney at the bottom is at least twice the width of the stack. The wider part is the back of the fireplace. On two-story homes when the wider portion continues at least halfway up the floor for the second story, suspect an additional fireplace, usually serving a family room or the master bedroom. Because each fireplace must have a separate flue, more than one flue at the top of the chimney is nearly diagnostic of an additional combustion appliance, most often another fireplace.
19. It should be noted that all rooms, regardless of size, use or the age of the house, are designed to reflect light and absorb sound. Consequently, lighter colors, especially whites, are preferred for reflecting light, and textured ceilings and walls, carpeted floors and drapes are preferred to absorb sound.

a small room opening on one end to the kitchen and on the other to the attached garage.

• Walk-in pantries are becoming more and more popular, especially in large, upscale houses. Pantry rooms are not only located near a kitchen, they are nearly always located immediately adjacent to them.

• Walk-in closets are most often found serving the master bedroom. To be usable, walk-in closets are a minimum of 3 feet 6 inches wide for a single closet and 5 feet 6 inches wide for a double closet.[20] Older walk-in closets use either swinging[21] or folding doors, and modern design uses either swinging doors or no door at all.

20. "Double closets" are simply closets with two clothes-hanging rails, open on both sides.
21. Swinging doors serving closets almost always swing out from the closet and into the room against a wall. Closets have no outside architectural features and must be determined by conjecture based upon their most likely shape and location.

CHAPTER 11

Extra Rooms, Upper Stories and Multiple Dwellings

For tactical diagramming purposes it would be nice if all dwellings were simple one-story rectangles. But houses are seldom perfectly rectangular, and two-story homes, town houses, apartments and condominiums are quite popular. Furthermore, additions, remodeling and modifications are common, especially on older buildings.[1] While this complicates the diagramming process, it in no way prevents it. As with all buildings, there are construction requirements and practices that, when known and understood, will provide strong clues to interior floor plans to include reconstruction and remodeling.

Additions

Americans have been adding onto, enlarging and remodeling[2] their homes from our earliest days. In fact, the older the structure the more likely it has undergone some type of reconstruction at least once in its lifetime. The most common type of addition is in some form of one or

---

1. In fact, the older the structure, the more likely it has undergone some reconstruction.
2. As noted in Chapter 4, it is important to understand the distinction between remodeling, renovating, and restoring. Remodeling involves reconstructing to enhance appearance, provide additional room and/or functions or adapting to a social change. Renovating involves modernizing a structure to update it and/or exploit new technologies and appliances. Restoring requires reconditioning or rejuvenating a structure to its original condition. Of the three, remodeling is not only the most common, but the most likely to affect floor plans and interior design.

more wings that protrude either perpendicular to the existing structure or from one end. The next most common is upper stories. Upper stories may cover an entire existing structure or just part of it. Bump-out additions are simply added onto a structure. They usually take the form of gable or shed dormers, car sheds and patios, but may less frequently be greenhouses, atriums and bay windows. The least common are wraparounds. These are almost always one-story additions added around two or more sides of two-story houses.

The first step in judging the impact an addition will have on an interior design is to determine whether it really is an addition. Many odd-shaped buildings and two-story houses were designed and built that way. Consequently, all existing diagramming rules apply for these structures. To identify an addition, look for any of the following:

- Obvious protrusions—Quite naturally, any protrusion from a building that seems out of place should heighten our suspicion that it was not part of the original design.
- Different styles—When compared to adjacent structures, a house that is conspicuously different, larger or smaller, or a different shape, should attract our interest.
- Asymmetrical design—Buildings are designed to be appealing; consequently, windows at different heights,[3] doors in odd places and other obvious peculiar architectural features should arouse our curiosity.
- Inappropriate landscaping—Because of the difficulty in relocating plants, especially trees, they may signal the presence of an addition.
- Different roof style, pitch or material—Roofs are expensive and constitute a major portion of the expense of an addition. As a result, one

---

3. Windows are installed "top down." This means that the tops of the windows are in alignment with each other, usually about 80 inches above the interior floors.

way of detecting an addition is looking to see if the roof has more than one pitch[4] or more than one color of roofing material.[5]

• Different colors of siding—Like roofing material, siding is expensive and difficult to closely match. This characteristic is particularly meaningful when the different colors of siding are in a vertical line, because siding is normally installed across the walls from the bottom up. As a result, there are never long vertical straight lines

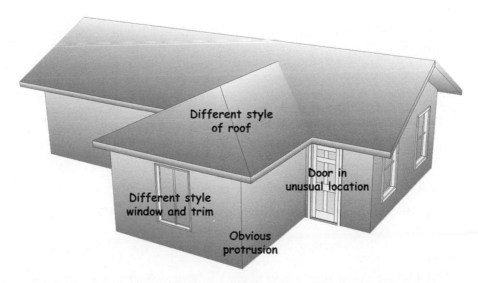

Figure 11.1 Addition, Wing: Determining whether an addition exists often requires identifying differences between the existing structure and the suspected addition and between the entire house and adjacent houses. In this illustration, four conspicuous clues that should arouse suspicion are the obvious protrusion from the side of the building coupled with a different style of roof, a door in an unusual location, and different styles of windows and trim. Other, more subtle corroborations might be shading differences in roofing or siding, unsightly seams in siding, inappropriate landscaping and so forth.

---

4. For a variety of reasons, additions often deviate from the original style or pitch of a roof. For example, many additions will use a shed roof attached to an original structure that has a gable roof.

5. Detecting more than one style or color of roofing material is not only a very good indicator of an addition, but can often identify a joint where an addition has been added. This is because roofing material tends to fade in the sun and even using the identical material to roof an addition often leaves a telltale line.

on properly installed siding. Other types of siding, like stucco, is likewise difficult to match identically and will frequently provide telltale "joints" where the newer stucco on the addition meets the older stucco of the original structure.

Once an addition has been identified, the next step is to ascertain what type of room or rooms were added. The best indicator for this is to identify what portion of the structure the addition is connected to.[6] Additions connected to sleeping areas are predominately bedrooms. If the addition is large enough, look also for a bathroom and closet space. Additions connected to living areas tend to be family rooms, romper rooms, and sometimes a home office. In some climates, patios and porches are enclosed to make "sun rooms." Additions connected to a food preparation area can either enlarge a kitchen or add a breakfast nook or dining area. When examining additions for other clues, all the building requirements and practices applicable to the original structure will still apply. To diagram them, simply apply the same rules to the addition, particularly those applicable to the portion of the house where the addition is attached.

Upper Stories

Like additions, upper stories tend to complicate the diagramming process because they obscure many useful architectural features located on the lower floors. Nevertheless, features on the upper floors can provide strong clues to the floor plan of the lower floors because the need to transfer the load through the strong vertical framing members results in a building practice of putting load-bearing walls over one another. Consequently, identifying a wall that transfers loads on one floor means one can reliably predict another load-bearing wall above or below it. This concept can be easily observed using the Window Alignment Rule, which states that, *with*

---

6. As discussed previously, houses can be generally divided into three components. These are the living area, sleeping area and food preparation area. See Chapter 5 for more information.

few exceptions, windows are installed from the top down and over one another. Thus even the tallest apartment building will have the windows in perfect alignment along the top and sides, over one another from the bottom of the building to the top,[7] and the floor plan for one floor will be very similar to the ones immediately above and below.

Plumbing is a considerable portion of construction expenses, and a practice of locating water appliances over one another is nearly universal. This is because water appliance vents are hidden in walls, and those located on lower floors must travel through walls in upper stories to reach the roof. Because of the difficulty and added construction cost in routing rigid pipes around obstacles, the vents tend to run from bottom to top in a straight line—so not only water appliance vents, but also the walls that contain the vents, are usually located directly over one another. Thus, while stack vents[8] are nearly worthless in determining the locations of walls on one-story buildings, their value increases considerably in multi-story buildings. Accordingly, the two rooms that require the most plumbing, bathrooms and kitchens, tend to be over one another in apartments, hotels, motels[9] and even office buildings.

Stairways[10] to upper floors are part of an exit system[11] and are heavily regulated by building codes. In houses, this has resulted in stairways being located immediately adjacent to the front entrance door.[12] In larger buildings, they terminate in a fire escape door and are located over one another. Consequently, once a stairway is located on one floor it is nearly certain that it will continue through the floors above and below it.

---

7. Some multi-story buildings use the first floor for retail space. Consequently, a different window pattern can be observed because the added construction cost is outweighed by the need for more window display area.
8. For more information on stack vents, see Chapter 7.
9. Building codes don't distinguish between motels and hotels, and the only significant difference in diagramming them is that hotels commonly use an inside public hallway, while motels use an outside walkway, often in the form of a balcony.
10. This includes elevators and fire stairs for commercial buildings.
11. For more information on exit systems, see Chapter 8.
12. Because of their rarity, spiral and circular staircases are not described here. Nevertheless, the same diagramming principles will apply.

Figure 11.2 Outside Staircase: Large, older houses are often converted to multiple dwellings. The addition of an outside staircase, as shown here, should be considered conclusive that the original building has been divided into more than one dwelling. While diagramming rules still apply, more caution needs to be exercised since "work arounds" are often necessary to put a kitchen upstairs, convert a bedroom into a living area, and the like.

While this pattern is not as rigidly adhered to in houses, it is still common for the stairway to the basement to be located under the stairs to the second story.[13] This is not so much regulated as a building practice because there is a lot of waste room under a stairway and it is most efficiently utilized over or under another stairway.[14]

Because of the requirements set forth by building codes, coupled with

---

13. Most building codes will also require a door at the entrance to the basement stairway. This is common for both residential and commercial construction.
14. Another very common use for the space under a stairway in a house is for closet space. In multi-story buildings, however, this space is required to remain open and unused to prevent the storage of combustible material that would block the fire escape.

efficient building practices, windows, plumbing and stairs can be used to facilitate tactical diagramming for two reasons. First, once they are identified, they provide strong clues as to what is most likely above and below them. In fact, they are so reliable that the architectural features identifying them on one floor can be used to predict where they will occur on the floors above and below them. Second, each of these building components comes with its own requirements. The end result is that the floor plans for large multiple-story buildings tend to be similar, if not the same.

Two-story buildings, especially single-family homes, do not rigidly follow this practice. Notwithstanding, there are some standard building practices that will greatly simplify tactical diagramming. These are:

- Kitchens are almost never found upstairs in single-family dwellings.
- Most, if not all, of the second story in single-family houses is used as a sleeping area. While this will normally include one or two bathrooms and perhaps a family room, the predominant use is for bedrooms. Bathrooms are not as common on the second story for houses older than about 1950.[15]
- Bathrooms on upper floors tend to be over bathrooms on lower floors.[16]
- The upper portion of stairways commonly terminates into a family room in contemporary two-story homes, and into a hallway that accesses bedrooms in older homes.
- Skylights, like windows, tend to be located in the center of rooms. While this is not a rigid rule, you can be certain that they will not be located over interior walls.
- Balconies and fireplaces[17] on second stories almost always indicate a family room or the master bedroom.

---

15. This does not include those houses where the second story was added on.
16. This principle holds true whether the building is a single-family house or a multiple-dwelling, multiple-story apartment building, hotel, motel or condominium.
17. For more information on fireplaces, see Chapter 7.

Multiple Dwellings

While the focus of this book is on houses, there has been a strong trend in recent years for multiple-family dwellings, especially in the form of townhouses and apartment buildings.[18] The primary reason is that when land became more expensive, the buildings on them needed to become more efficient. As a result, apartments, condominiums and townhouses have been increasing in popularity, and newlyweds today are more likely to begin their life together in one of these than in the smaller houses purchased or rented by their parents and grandparents. While hotels and motels are not usually considered dwellings, they do offer temporary housing, and accordingly, many of the diagramming principles described in this section will also apply to them.

Nearly all multiple dwellings take on one of three configurations. They are described in the order of difficulty for tactical diagramming below.

The first type is a one- or two-story building containing two or more dwellings. These buildings are most often referred to as duplexes, or in some cases triplexes. Many buildings of this type began their life in the earlier part of the century as large single-family houses. When the owners wanted to move away or the buildings became too expensive to maintain, they were subdivided into two or three smaller residences. Because by definition they have been remodeled and/or renovated, they present formidable challenges to tactical diagramming.

The second type is the townhouse. Townhouses are buildings in which each residence is a separate dwelling but connected by common sidewalls. In their earlier forms they were called row houses, and in some parts of the country they are still referred to by that name. Nevertheless, contemporary construction practices seldom have them in perfectly straight rows, and they are just as apt to be found in the outlying metropolitan areas as they are in the central city. They frequently

---

18. For more information on housing trends, see Chapter 4.

have balconies and/or very small backyards or atriums but almost never separate yards. While not as difficult to diagram as the first type, they are more difficult than apartments.

The third form is the multiple-apartment building.[19] These buildings are usually two (but on occasion, three or more) stories tall. They are constructed in areas zoned specifically for multiple dwellings and as a result tend to be adjacent to one another rather than to other houses. In the central portions of larger cities, these buildings can also take the form of skyscrapers[20] and can be 10 or more stories tall. Of the three forms of multiple-dwelling structures, apartments are usually the easiest to diagram for reasons that will become apparent later in this section.[21]

Condominiums, sometimes called "condos," may resemble either a multiple-apartment building or a townhouse. This is because a condominium describes more a style of ownership than a style of building in that title is conferred individually to the dwelling, but common elements, such as yards, playgrounds, parks, streets, sidewalks, and sometimes garages and parking areas are jointly owned.

Of the three types, duplexes and triplexes are by far the most difficult to diagram. This is particularly so when they are subdivisions of an older house, because the structure had to be remodeled, not only to accommodate the walls separating the two dwellings, but extra doors, bathrooms and kitchens. The most effective method for diagramming these difficult buildings has been to incorporate all the diagramming

---

19. While apartment buildings are comprised of separate residences, they are often connected by a common attic. This can be crucial when a suspect escapes into an attic because he can enter another apartment through the ceiling. Generally, attics for buildings of this type must be partitioned only if they exceed 3,000 square feet.

20. Multiple-dwelling skyscrapers represent a very small percentage of the dwellings in the United States but are more frequent in other parts of the world. They are of relatively recent construction, with the oldest being the Home Insurance Building in Chicago, constructed in 1885. Their use primarily as dwellings is even more recent, almost all within the last three or four decades.

21. Hotels and motels also fall within this category.

principles based upon the visible architectural features while keeping in mind how the original floor plan must have originally appeared. Here are some useful building practices for duplexes and triplexes:

- When multiple residences are suspected, look for duplicates of electrical and water meters, mail boxes or mail slots, front doors, doorbells, newspapers and other deliveries, and don't overlook the obvious duplicate street numbers on the same building.
- The separation between the dwellings is usually the floors themselves, since all that is required is to remove the stairway between the floors. The stairway space is then most often converted to closets. Look for an upstairs entrance door, usually very conspicuous because of the necessity for an outside stairway.
- Two-story conversion duplexes have had to add a kitchen upstairs. This is most cheaply done by locating it over the existing downstairs kitchen, but when this is not possible, a bedroom must be converted. The vent pipes, drains and other required plumbing are sometimes routed along the outside of the exterior walls to avoid demolishing and rebuilding large sections of walls.
- Because of the difficulty and added expense, single-story houses that have been subdivided seldom move bearing walls. Thus the separation is often an existing bearing wall. Look for entrance doors on either side of where you expect a bearing wall.[22]
- Duplexes and triplexes that were specifically built for that purpose have either identical floor plans or reverse floor plans.[23]

---

22. For more information on bearing walls, see Chapter 5.
23. This is also very common for single-family tract homes. While the outside appearance may be dramatically altered by changing the shape of the roof, color and style of the siding, landscaping etc., the floor plans can be identical. To determine which buildings use the same floor plans, look for vent patterns, window sizes and patterns, masonry chimneys, garage doors and so forth. The more similarities exist between two structures (including mirror images), the more likely it is that they are using the same (or reverse) floor plan. When used appropriately, this method can be diagnostic.

Multiple electrical and water meters

Figure 11.3 Townhouses and Condominiums: All the rules for diagramming single-family dwellings apply to multiple dwellings, such as this large condominium. The presence of multiple electrical, gas or water meters, multiple mailboxes, mail slots, and other obvious indicators may help identify the number of dwellings. Additionally, besides the practice of writing the tenant's name on a mailbox, it is a common habit of public utilities to write the name of the tenant on a tag on a meter, or even the meter itself, when service is turned. Thus the precise apartment or room number of a target location may be determined.

The second type of multiple dwelling is the townhouse variety. The townhouse is popular with city dwellers for two primary reasons. First, it provides all the comforts of a house at a substantially reduced price. Second, a homeowner's association provides the routine home maintenance, such as lawn mowing and hedge trimming, as well as some repairs. Participation in the association is mandatory, so neighbors with sloppy or lazy habits are prompted by policy to avoid a rundown neighborhood. In the same manner, requirements for the construction of out buildings, patios, gazebos, and the like must conform to the association's rules, to include materials, style and even color.

While townhouses are frequently two-story structures, they are vastly easier to diagram than subdivided duplexes and triplexes because they were built specifically as single-family residences. Consequently, all the diagramming principles that apply to other single-family residences are also applicable. Furthermore, the most common style of a townhouse project is to have four or five designs and then repeat them throughout the tract. This means that architectural features of other buildings can be used to predict the floor plan for a target. The value of this technique for features that are obscured by trees or other buildings, or in defilade behind another structure, hardly needs comment. Even better, large tracts may allow a "walk through" at a distant but identical structure without alerting suspects. Here are some useful techniques for diagramming townhouses:

- One of the easiest methods of determining which structures use identical floor plans is to examine the vent and window patterns. This method is easily accomplished and nearly foolproof.[24]
- Townhouse owners are required to belong to a homeowner's association that provides for the common good and maintenance of joint property. Because they tend to be very conservative, it is all but impossible to obtain approval for remodeling, especially for anything that will change the appearance of the structure. This simplifies diagramming, even on older townhouses.
- Because townhouses are connected to one another, fire in one dwelling threatens the others. Consequently, the local jurisdiction often regulates them more strictly than single-family houses and may require a fire plan, complete with blueprints, identifying fire escapes, fire hoses etc., that may provide a bounty of diagramming information. Local planning or building departments may have blueprints on file.

---

24. For more information on vent patterns, see Chapter 7. For more information on window installations, see Chapter 9.

- Contractors and building speculators who build these tracts often reuse the plans for other tracts. The identity of the contractor or building company who erected the townhouses is usually on file with the local planning or building department, and a quick phone call may be all that is needed to obtain a complete floor plan.

Tactical diagrams for multiple-apartment buildings, hotels or motel are relatively easy to obtain for several reasons. First, because these are high-density buildings subject to numerous restrictions and inspections, it is almost always possible to get a look inside using an inspection as a pretense. Second, local jurisdictions frequently have floor plans on file for a variety of reasons, not the least of which is fire planning. Third, virtually all of them use a floor plan model called a **reverse floor plan**. This is for a variety of reasons, but one of the main ones is to take advantage of a common wall to hold the plumbing for more than one dwelling, frequently the one that separates the dwellings. This not only allows a common drainage and vent system but is frequently doubled in thickness to provide sound insulation between dwellings. This provides us with a useful diagramming rule called the Mirror Rule, which states that *separate dwellings in multiple-dwelling structures tend to use reverse floor plans, which are mirror images of those adjacent.*[25] Furthermore, tract homes use only about four floor plans. Regardless of the number of different structures, each has one of the four original plans, or a reverse of it.

There are generally three conventions for identifying individual dwellings that are using the same floor plans. The first is for numbering the individual floors. This is usually done with a "1" followed by a two-digit numeric identifier for each room, and so on through all the floors. For

---

25. While there are some exceptions, the most common is the rooms at the ends of the buildings. Even these, however, tend to be identical or mirror images of their counterparts on the other end of the building.

Figure 11.4 Reverse Floor Plans: Builders often change the appearance of houses, sometimes dramatically, by simply changing the roof style, siding or landscaping. At first glance, these six houses all appear unique, but a skilled tactical diagrammer will note subtle similar patterns in windows, doors, vents and so forth. In point of fact, all six of these houses share either the same floor plan or the reverse of it. This practice is especially common in multiple dwellings such as apartments, condominiums or townhouses. Once this practice is identified, it allows the features of one building to be used to predict the floor plans of another. In separate dwellings, it may even allow a "walk through" at a distant but identical building to yield insight that no amount of diagramming can ever provide.

example, apartment 403 would be the third apartment on the fourth floor.[26] The second is a convention for identifying the individual rooms on each floor, which tends to be either odd numbers on one side of a hallway and even numbers on the other, or a circular plan, either clockwise or counter-clockwise.[27] Less frequently, a sequential system is used beginning at an entrance. After determining the numbering convention, it is a simple matter to identify the apartments above and below that are using the identical floor plan and in most cases, those on the same floor.[28] For example, room num-

---

26. In North America, the ground floor is considered the first floor, but in Europe the first floor is considered the one above the ground floor.
27. The numbering system usually begins at an entrance or elevator or one end of a building.
28. For example, room numbers 205, 305, 405 and so forth will almost always use the same floor plan. Likewise, the even numbered rooms on either side of these rooms will be mirror images.

bers "205," "305," "405" and so forth, will almost always use the same floor plan. Likewise, the even numbered rooms on either side of these rooms will be mirror images. Some helpful aids for diagramming these structures are:

- These buildings have public corridors to gain access to the separate residences. Most fire codes will require a fire escape plan to be posted near fire stairs and elevators. These will identify the individual residences, fire escapes and other important diagramming information.
- Building diagrams can often be obtained at the counter of hotels and motels in the form of handouts or brochures because they are needed to provide directions for guests. While they tend to be coarse, providing only general information, they can be a great aid in identifying a target and those rooms using the same floor plan.
- Because doors may not reduce the required width of a public corridor by more than 7 inches when fully opened, they will swing into the individual residences.[29] Doors may swing into the hallway if they do not obstruct more than half the corridor in any position. They may also be set into insets called "door wells" to comply with this requirement. This is not very common because the floor space necessary to open the door is wasted since it can't be used for anything else.
- For fire escapes, only bedrooms below the fourth floor are required to have an openable window. While normally much larger, these windows must be at least 24 inches high by 20 inches wide and no more than 44 inches above the floor.[30]
- All corridors must terminate in a cross-aisle, foyer or exit, and no corridor can have a dead-end length of more than 20 feet to avoid people becoming lost or trapped in an emergency.

---

29. Doors may swing into the hallway if they do not obstruct more than half the corridor in any position. While not common, they may be set into insets called **door wells** to comply with this requirement. For more information on doors, see Chapter 8.
30. Floors above the fourth floor are normally excluded because that's about as high as most fire department ladders can reach.

CHAPTER 12

Saved Rounds

At the end of a Marine Corps briefing or debriefing the meeting leader often ends with the question, "Any saved rounds?" On the rifle range (where Marines spend a substantial amount of time) a "saved round" refers to an unfired round that, for one reason or another, was legitimately not fired and the shooter is allowed to fire it for qualification. In a briefing or debriefing, it refers to items and issues that were not part of the agenda but that need to be brought up for consideration or notice. So it is that at the end of this book I have several "saved rounds" that need to be described but did not neatly fit in with any of the chapter subjects.

Obtaining Intelligence for Diagramming

The first rule in obtaining the information necessary to create reliable tactical diagrams is to get it yourself! Naturally, good arguments can be made, especially for warrant service operations, for detectives to provide the necessary photographs and sketches. This method is based on the belief that because detectives are more familiar with a case, especially narcotics officers with relaxed grooming standards, they are less likely to be compromised and alert the suspects. On rare occasions, this may be necessary, but diagrams suffer, often dramatically, from a lack of firsthand information. While detectives are trained investigators and may have spent weeks or months investigating a case, their orientation is on evidence gathering for prosecution. Tactical personnel are focused on interventions and will look at the structure and terrain with a much different perspective.

This concept is easily demonstrated when negotiators and tactical personnel are dealing with a barricaded suspect on a telephone. The negotiators are keenly listening for clues to determine things like whether the suspect is rational, under the influence of drugs or agitated, if there is more than one suspect, and if so, are they talking to the "shot caller" or an underling? Tactical personnel want to know where the phone is, since it precisely places the suspect inside a room.[1] Likewise, photographs taken by detectives used to obtain a search or arrest warrant will focus on the color of the siding, roofing, curb markings and other features needed to precisely identify a building. Tactical diagrammers will be focused on seeing through windows, locating vents, identifying similar adjacent structures, and the like.

The information needed to create reliable tactical diagrams comes in all sorts of forms but is usually in the form of photographs. While these photographs may be obtained in any number of ways, they are predominately during "drive-bys" and "fly-bys."

Drive-by Photographs

Drive-by photographs, as the name implies, are obtained by simply driving by a target location and taking pictures. This is easy in concept and difficult in application for several reasons. First, being seen taking pictures of a location, even by an unsuspecting neighbor, is likely to alert the suspect that something is up. Furthermore, taking pictures surreptitiously, especially through window glass, often degrades the quality of the photographs. Second, more than one pass is often needed, because many warrant services are conducted in the early morning hours but daylight is needed to identify and locate the architectural features necessary

---

1. With the popularity of cordless and cell phones, this is becoming increasingly less reliable.

for diagramming. And, because the situation at a residence will change by the time of day when vehicles are home or missing, doors are shut or open, dogs are tied up or loose, etc., an additional pass will be necessary near the planned time of the warrant service to incorporate the changes into the diagram and tactical plan. Third, some architectural features are better seen in bright sunlight, others in low light, especially dusk, and in the northern climates, especially when snow is on the ground, a house can be silhouetted by a low sun, making it nearly impossible to distinguish the features necessary for diagramming.

Like any other part of a tactical operation, the drive-by needs to be planned. Many houses look alike, especially in tracts. Besides planning when to do a drive-by, it is necessary to determine how to precisely identify the target. When this might be difficult, prominent terrain features provide advantages over the address numbers on houses and curbs since they can be seen from a greater distance and will not require staring intently or lingering near the target. When choosing a camera and film, a 35mm camera equipped with a zoom telephoto from about 80 to 210mm will provide an ability to take a perspective view and then quickly zoom in on a small architectural feature for later viewing. The film needs to be quite fast to allow a faster shutter speed, photography in low light and through tinted glass. Generally, a 400 ASA film speed provides excellent results, but occasionally 800 ASA, or even faster, is necessary. As digital cameras are becoming more efficient and available, a high speed processor coupled with a dense format (five or more megapixels) is even better.

By far, the most common method for conducting a drive-by is a single vehicle, often a van that is nondescript in color and markings. Vans have proven especially useful because they allow the photographers to remain hidden while taking pictures through side windows as the driver slows down without stopping. All efforts should be made to obtain all the necessary photographs with a single pass, but under no circumstances should the vehicle stop or loiter near the target without a plausible reason. On the rare occasion when it is necessary for the photographing vehicle to stop or loiter near the target, a "lead car" in front that attracts attention with engine trouble, by appearing to look for an address, or by any number of ploys, will help to focus attention on itself instead of the van behind it. This works best when the lead vehicle allows a clear view inside, has no passengers, and the driver "fits" the area or is a lone female.

Fly-by Photographs

As with drive-bys, the fly-by method takes its name from the method by which it is accomplished. While fly-bys are normally done with a helicopter, they have also been done using advertising blimps, fixed-wing private planes, and even satellites. Nowadays, in fact, commercial satellite photographs are available directly from the Internet for as little as $35 to $50, but $200 to $800 will be nearer the price for recent, high-quality photographs with enough clear detail to enable reliable operational planning. That said, those available free from sites like MSR Maps, Google Maps, and the United States Geological Survey are becoming more and more useful and will provide a wealth of useful diagramming information. None, however, can provide the same degree of detail of a fly-by specifically focused on gathering information for tactical diagramming.

When conducting a fly-by, choose a clear day and an altitude of between 500 and 1,500 feet AGL (above ground level). An altitude lower than 500 feet is sure to draw attention, and the farther above 1,500 feet, the more difficult it is to identify and photograph the smaller architectural features. As with drive-bys, timing is important. While noon is best for reducing the effects of shadows, some architectural features are so difficult to detect that their shadows are more conspicuous than they are. Water appliance vents are one good example because their profile from the air is very small and they are often painted the same color as the roof. Because of their diagramming significance it is well worth the extra effort of determining their precise location. Consequently, a fly-by in the early morning or late afternoon when their shadows are larger makes them easier to detect.

More than one camera—and, whenever possible, more than one photographer—is a boon to fly-by photos. A 35mm camera with an 80 to 300mm zoom lens is a good investment because the shorter focal length will allow a perspective that can be used to plan avenues of approach for convoys and allow the identification of avenues of approach and escape. The longer focal length helps to capture smaller details for closer examination later. Photographing from the air also requires a filter to reduce the bluish-green effects in the photograph. A skylight 1A or 1B filter is inexpensive, protects the lens and reduces the false color. Unlike drive-bys, fly-by photographs need a slower film speed, 100 ASA to 200 ASA. The slower film speeds allow enlargement without a grainy effect while still providing a shutter speed of 1/250th of a second or faster. The faster shutter speeds reduce the effects of the jarring in the helicopter while still allowing clear photographs.[2] Regardless of whether the photography is done on the ground or in the air, the film is the cheapest part. Take lots of pictures from as many different perspectives as the tactical situation will allow.

Worth mentioning here is the use of digital photographs. Digital photography offers many advantages over the conventional photographs that most of us have become accustomed to, especially in price. Likewise, a dense digital photo can be greatly enlarged ("zoomed") to examine small details. Nevertheless, they are not without trade-offs. For example, only the best (and most expensive) digital cameras are

---

2. On many smaller helicopters the doors are easily removed. This allows photographing through the opening without glare or reflection.

capable of processing repeated exposures as fast as a film camera, especially when the images are extremely fine (dense) to enable enlargement for close examination. Regardless, digital photography is becoming the new standard and has already largely replaced the conventional methods currently in use for all but photography aficionados. When choosing a digital camera for surveillance photographs, three features have emerged as critical. The first is that it needs to be able to capture images of at least five megapixels. This will allow clear prints, enlargements and magnified electronic scrutiny without surrendering huge amounts of detail when the picture becomes grainy. The second feature is that it needs a strong optical zoom, at least 7-power, to provide an ability to zoom in on critical features. Do not be confused with a "digital zoom," because anything you can do digitally on a camera, you can also do faster and more easily on your computer when you later examine the photographs. Finally, it needs a fast recycle rate. Cheaper cameras and high-density photographs can take 15 seconds or longer to process. While a slow recycling rate is a nuisance in most instances, it is a major encumbrance when trying to remain inconspicuous during a reconnaissance or surveillance.

It is important to remember that it is easier to compromise an operation if a fly-by is detected than if a drive-by is detected. Many vehicles will routinely drive by a suspect's house for all manner of reasons, but a helicopter loitering above a target location automatically attracts attention and is much harder to explain away. Consequently, extra care must be taken to avoid alerting suspects to a raid. One of the best methods to obtain the necessary photographs is using an L-shaped flight path. This allows all four sides of a building to be photographed in a single pass. It begins with an offset approach from one of the four sides using a telephoto lens. As the helicopter draws abreast of the target, the next side is exposed. Finally, as the helicopter turns behind the target the last two sides are exposed during the withdrawal. In this manner, all four

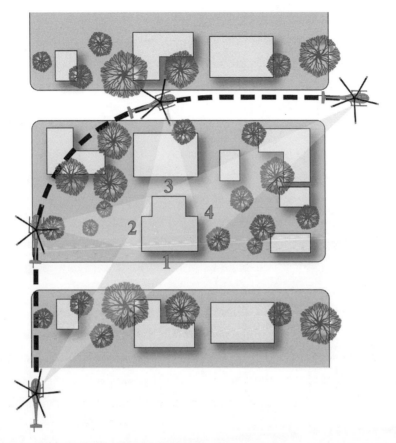

Figure 12.1 Fly-by: An "L-shaped" flight path allows aerial observation and photography of all four sides of a target location in a single pass. Consequently, it greatly reduces the chances of compromising an operation by leery suspects while gathering needed intelligence and photographs for tactical diagramming and planning purposes.

sides of a location can be observed and photographed without circling or loitering. If another pass is necessary, it can be conducted in reverse later to avoid alerting wary suspects.[3]

As any pilot or aerial observer will attest, locating a specific building from the air is much harder than when on the ground. It is especially

---

3. Years of personal experience have shown that it is not uncommon for major drug dealers to install an "air sentry" who is paid to watch for helicopters loitering around drug caches or sales and distribution locations.

difficult with houses and buildings constructed in tracts. Locating a specific building in a "sea of buildings" is normally done by using two navigation methods. First, cardinal directions are used to get into the general area, and then the observer can "shift from a known point" to precisely identify a target.

Cardinal directions will allow a pilot to move from an airport or landing zone to a general area, especially if he or she is familiar with the region. Afterwards, however, locating a specific house or building is the responsibility of the tactical observer. It goes without saying that street addresses are nearly worthless. Consequently, prominent terrain features[4] are used to narrow the search. The most common method is to begin with the most conspicuous prominent terrain features, such as road intersections, rivers, conspicuous buildings and the like, and then identify those specific to a target location to precisely identify a particular building. These features need to be chosen with care so that they are not only recognizable from the air but also precise to the location. Examples might be "the third house east of the intersection" or "the only two-story house on the north side of the street," etc. On rare occasions it has been necessary to coordinate the fly-by photography with a ground unit that is followed to a target location from the air and "marks" the target verbally using a cell phone or radio.

Reverse Diagramming

Like drive-bys and fly-bys, reverse diagramming takes its name from the method by which it is accomplished. Rather than determining floor plans from outside architectural features, reverse diagramming uses inside fixtures and furniture to determine the size and shape of the rooms, which are then used to diagram the entire building. It goes without saying that this method has limited applications in tactical situations

---

4.   For more information on prominent terrain, see Chapter 2.

given that it is necessary to gain entry to get the necessary information. Even so, it can be a valuable tool because many floor plans are repeated throughout tract homes, condominiums, townhouses, hotels, motels and apartment buildings. Accordingly, an examination of one location can be used to diagram another.

The essential information for reverse diagramming often results from interviews of informants or undercover police officers who have been inside a location, or even at another location with the same floor plan. It works for the same reason that tactical diagramming works because furniture and fixtures, like outside architectural features are common in size and use. A toilet, for example, is "size small, fits all." Likewise, bathtubs, sinks, televisions, couches, chairs and most everything else comes in standard sizes. Even when there are different dimensions, the differences are insignificant when determining rough floor plans. When interviewing people who have actually been inside a location, have them sketch in the furniture. A simple review of any furniture catalog then provides the sizes. The fact that they are not known precisely is of little consequence because the few inches' difference between furniture sizes has almost no effect on the actual diagram.

When constructing a reverse diagram, simply draw the furniture to scale and in the approximate distribution and arrangement remembered. Then draw the walls around it. The use of a computer tremendously facilitates this process. The end results can be easily seen in Figure 12.2. This is an actual diagram from a tactical operation in 1987 that resulted in the arrests of three torture/murder suspects for hire. A reliable diagram was critical to the operation because it was impossible to evacuate the tenants without alerting the suspects, and so closely controlled avenues of approach, sectors of fire and gun target lines were imperative.

After the initial diagram of the rooms was completed, the extraneous information was deleted and the outline of the rooms was then

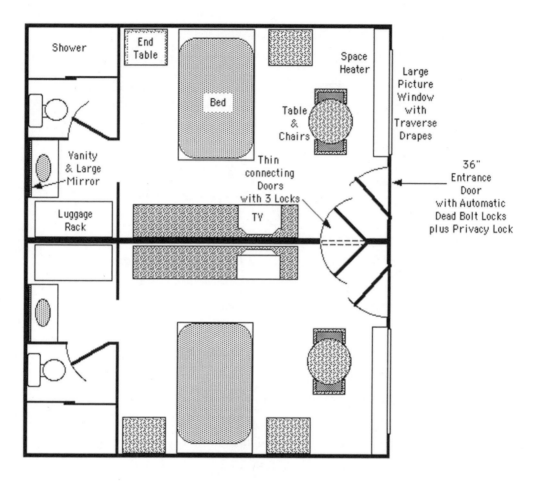

Connecting Rooms are Mirror Images of each other.

Figure 12.2 Reverse Diagramming—Room: This is an actual diagram conducted in reverse. The operation required the safe capture of three torture and murder suspects in a large motel. Two undercover police officers had asked to see a room under pretense of renting a block of rooms for an upcoming conference. After they viewed the room and memorized the furniture, a Sears catalog provided the critical dimensions. Note that the rooms are mirror images of each other. This is very common in large apartment buildings, motels, hotels and so forth. The fact that the operation occurred in 1987 shows the degree of sophistication tactical diagramming had reached even then.

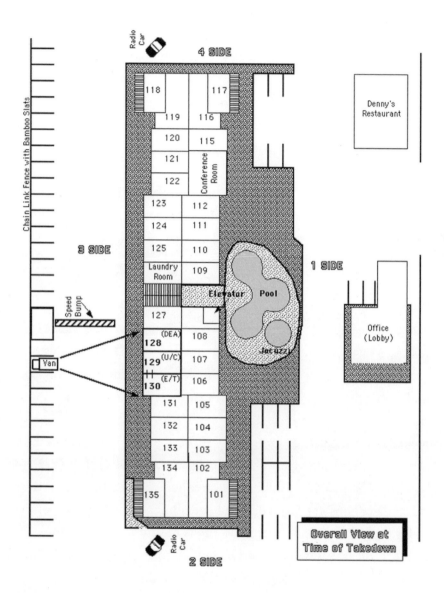

Figure 12.3 Reverse Diagramming—Building: Once the individual room was diagrammed (in this case a duplicate of room 130), a computer was used to place each of the other rooms in the appropriate relationship based upon photographs and surveillance of the outside architectural features. This eventually yielded the building and grounds as shown. Note the identified micro and prominent terrain such as the Denny's restaurant, motel office, chain link fence, building stairwells, speed bump and odd-shaped swimming pool.

copied and pasted to create a diagram of the entire structure (Figure 12.3). The initial diagram sketch was then compared with surveillance photographs and adjusted accordingly to include stairwells, elevators, pools and so forth in the same manner as conventional diagramming. Note here that prominent terrain features with seemingly little tactical value, such as the odd-shaped pool and speed bump, were added for navigation purposes.

Once the methods for conventional diagramming are mastered, reverse diagramming is a relatively simple procedure, and while its use is somewhat rare, its value can be substantial.

Factory-Built Homes

When this book was first outlined, factory-built houses were assigned their own chapter. As the research became more focused, however, it was clear that the principles for diagramming other types of dwellings were nearly identical for factory-built homes. While there are some small differences, they are so slight that they need only be mentioned and do not merit an entire chapter.

Factory-built homes are simply those that are manufactured in a factory and assembled on a building site. Generally, there are four varieties. The panelized method is so called because the walls, floors and roof sections are framed in the conventional manner but off-site, exploiting the mass production methods of any modern factory. The walls are sheathed on the exterior, but the interior sides are left open to allow the installation of insulation, plumbing and wiring at the building site. The modular method is similar, but instead of just the components, entire rooms and wings are constructed. This method exploits not only the mass production of a factory, but also modern transportation on flatbed trucks and railroad cars that can transport components up to about 14 feet wide and 60 feet long. When using this method, most of the details, such as wiring, plumbing, insula-

Figure 12.4 Factory-Built Homes: The easiest method of determining whether a house is factory-built is to identify an adjacent house that is also factory-built, since this type tends to be clustered because of local building codes and zoning ordinances. The house in the top photo is clearly using the modular method and is sitting on jacks until a permanent concrete-block footing can be installed to support it. A close examination of the photo on the bottom will reveal that this house is also sitting on a raised foundation that has been cleverly concealed with siding. In particular, note the raised porch to access the front door.

tion and wall coverings, are already installed. The third method calls for SIPs, which is an acronym for Structural Insulated Panels. This method is not so much a new method as an improvement on the panelized method. The panels comprise the walls and floors and include the exterior sheathing and foam insulation, and are then assembled on the job site. The fourth type is the so-called "mobile home."[5] I say so-called because they are not as mobile as most would think.

------

5. While the term "mobile home" is still common, the term "manufactured home" has been the legal definition since the U.S. Congress passed the National Manufactured Housing Construction and Safety Act (42 U.S.C.) to enforce manufacturing standards. Technically, only those homes built prior to this are still considered "mobile homes."

The majority of mobile homes are built and moved from the factory to a building site or mobile home park and then never moved again. Of the four types, the floor plan of a mobile home is the easiest to determine because these homes tend to be elongated rectangles to facilitate movement on the roads. Thus a "double-wide"[6] is simply two rectangles placed side by side.

Factory-built homes can be assembled much more quickly than site-built homes and are popular where construction schedules that are affected by harsh weather or other constraints require a minimum of disruption or time at job sites. Even so, they do not allow versatility of design, and on-

Figure 12.5 Trailer Park: Many building and zoning codes "cluster" these types of homes next to one another, as in this "trailer park." While the sizes are nearly all similar, brands, styles, and floor plans can differ substantially from one another. Hence, floor plans obtained from adjacent structures are not as reliable as they would be with tract homes. Even so, all other tactical diagramming techniques are applicable.

---

6. The term "double-wide" is used in the mobile home industry to identify a home that is constructed by installing two modules, each slender enough to traverse conventional roadways, side by side at a building site. Thus the final structure is "double wide."

site modifications can be difficult or even impossible. Consequently, they have not competed well with conventional construction.[7]

Determining whether a house you are diagramming has been factory-built is difficult because the differences are so slight from conventional methods. Some useful indications are when other houses in the same tract have already been identified as factory-built, when partially constructed homes are clearly constructed from modules or panels, when a house is raised above the ground for no apparent reason,[8] and other features that are seemingly incongruent with conventional construction.

Other Countries

One question that often arises is "Will tactical diagramming work in other countries?" The answer is a qualified yes. I say qualified, because while the overall method is applicable, the building codes, methods and principles can vary dramatically according to culture, climate and building materials. During the first Gulf War, for example, we noted that the Kuwaiti houses almost never had bedroom closets but opted for the European-style armoire.[9] Furthermore, interior pocket doors were as popular as the swinging type. During the second Gulf War we noted that nearly every Iraqi house had an open veranda on the top. In the Balkans we noted that most of the houses were built of timbers with the spaces filled in with concrete blocks, thus reducing the need for interior bearing walls. The best advice for diagramming in a different country or culture is to observe similar

---

7. Factory-built homes represent less than 10 percent of the residential construction market. (Gibson, Scott, "Factory-Built Houses," *Fine Homebuilding*, June–July 2004, p. 56)
8. While "raised platform" construction is not uncommon, it is conspicuous because the footings and foundation are almost always of concrete, concrete blocks, or other masonry. Manufactured housing usually covers the building supports with the same siding as the remainder of the structure.
9. An armoire is a large, cabinet-like wardrobe. It was also popular in the United States throughout the nineteenth century but fell from favor and has been almost entirely replaced by built-in closets.

structures, because the target is most likely to be constructed in the same manner and style.

Diagramming Tools

The tools necessary for tactical diagramming can be as simple as a lined notebook and a pencil or as complex as a computer with architectural software. For field use, 1/4-inch graph paper and a sharp pencil with #2 lead can produce some pretty handsome and reliable diagrams.[10] When time and the tactical situation permits, these can be augmented at a field command post with such tools as clipboards and rulers. Sketching right over photographs is also possible, especially with the popularity of digital cameras and plain-paper printers. But for really elegant diagrams, a computer and drawing software are unsurpassed. Some software can be learned in as little as an hour of practice and will produce not only scaled drawings but 3D depictions. This software will run on laptops and comes complete with electronic libraries of furniture, plants, building materials and tutorials.[11] Some will even allow a virtual "walk through" or "fly-by"!

Regardless of the configuration of computer and software, the ease with which computer-generated graphics can be duplicated, flipped, rotated, resized, redistributed and displayed and electronically transmitted will immensely simpifly the generation of elaborate and accurate tactical diagrams.

Finally

Many progressive tactical teams use diagrams in one form or another, but few have made the effort to become truly proficient. Excuses have

---

10. My personal preference is a mechanical pencil with .7mm HB lead and a mechanical plastic "eraser stick."
11. This book was largely illustrated using Home Design Architectural Series 4000™ from Punch Software.

ranged from "It takes too much time" to "It's not precise enough to rely on, so we'd rather not form any incorrect conclusions." Both of these arguments have merit on occasion but become quite shallow when used consistently. Throughout this book I have resisted the temptation to use personal anecdotes and "war stories" to emphasize how important a role tactical diagramming can play. Suffice it to say that I can personally attest to the success of a number of missions, and our survival on a few, because of the "inside information" we extrapolated from seemingly inconsequential observations. I take my greatest joy in the hope that this book will make some small contribution to that end for my comrades in arms.

Learn from the mistakes of others; you'll never live long enough to make them all yourself![12]

---

12. Taken from a sign over a paraloft while I was in the Marine Corps. Its meaning and significance should need no further explanation in a profession that chastens its failures with death.

Appendix A: Concept Glossary

Avenue of Approach and Escape—any route by which a force can reach a tactical objective. In the case of a suspect, this might mean escape. In the case of a tactical team, it might mean being able to reach a suspect's location, vantage point, place of cover or any other key terrain.

Barrier—any obstacle or terrain feature so formidable that it prevents movement. (see also *obstacle*)

Concealment—anything that prevents observation. Concealment may prevent a suspect from observing officers' movements but will not prevent injury if he fires at them. (see also *cover*)

Coup d'Oeil Concept—a French expression that, loosely translated, means the "strike of the eye" or the "vision behind the eye." The closest English concept would be that of intuition.

Cover—anything that provides protection against fires and the effects from fires. *Effects* from fires would include anything that can hurt you as a result of being shot at. (see also *concealment*)

Decisive Terrain—any terrain feature that offers a decisive advantage. It is also frequently referred to as "commanding terrain." (see also *key terrain*)

Dormer—a framed structure that projects from a roof surface to add space, light and ventilation to an attic area. They generally come in two styles identified by their roof styles. These are gable dormers and shed dormers.

Eave—the overhanging lower edge of a roof.

Exit System—any combination of doors, windows, hallways, or other architectural features designed to facilitate and expedite the evacuation of a building.

Field of Fire—the area that a weapon can cover effectively from a given position. This means that the characteristics of the weapon and how it is deployed define a field of fire. (see also *sector of fire*)

Gable—the triangle portion at each end of a building and any wing under a pitched roof. Sometimes the entire wall is called a "gable wall."

Key terrain—any locality, area or feature, the control of which offers a marked advantage to either you or a suspect. (see also *decisive terrain*)

Micro-terrain—terrain that will have an impact on a tactical operation but is too small or insignificant to be depicted on a map. (see also *prominent terrain*)

Observation—the surveillance that can be exercised either visually or through the use of optic or electronic devices.

Obstacle—any object or terrain feature that impedes or diverts movement in an area of operation. (see also *barriers*)

Pitch—the amount of slope of a roof. Pitch is expressed as the number of inches of vertical rise per foot. The greater the rise, the steeper the slope. For residences, this usually varies from a 4/12 to a 6/12 pitch, meaning that the roof rises either 4 or 6 inches for every 12 inches of horizontal distance.

Prominent Terrain—any terrain feature that can be easily identified and is displayed on a map. It is most often used to orient a person as to direction and distance. (see also *micro-terrain*)

Rafter—one of the sloping framing members that supports a pitched roof.

Reverse Diagramming—a process for determining floor plans that works from the inside out. Rather than determining floor plans from outside architectural features, reverse diagramming uses inside appliances, fixtures and furniture to determine the size and shape of the rooms, which are then used to diagram the entire building. While it is seldom used on houses it has advantages for motels, hotels, apartments, and other multiple dwelling structures.

Reverse Floor Plans—floor plans that are mirror images from those adjacent to them. This feature is common with many tract houses and virtually ubiquitous for motel and hotel rooms and apartments.

Ridge or Peak—the highest portion of a roof. Some roofs, especially hip roofs, have a peak with no ridge when all four sides slope to a single point, but most will have both a peak and a ridge, which is the line formed when two sides slope to the same line.

Sector of Fire—an assignment that defines the limits within which a weapon is allowed to be fired. (see also *field of fire*)

Span—the distance or measure of space between two supports. This could be between two walls, two posts, a post and a wall, or any combination. While design can influence the length of a span, spans are always limited, especially in wood frame construction. (see *Rule of 14*)

Stack Vent—a venting system that serves more than one water appliance to a single vent through the roof. Stack vent systems, sometimes called *common vent systems*, always use a larger pipe than single-appliance vents and have limited diagramming value.

Stud—a vertical framing member used in the construction of buildings used to support walls. Most studs are 2 x 4s, but 2 x 6s and even 2 x 8s may be required for multi-story buildings.

Terrain Analysis—the process by which critical terrain features are identified and evaluated for their impact on a tactical operation. The most common method involves a five-step process identified by the acronym KOCOA. This stands for:

- **K**ey Terrain Features (sometimes referred to as **C**ritical Terrain Features)
- **O**bservation and Fields of Fire
- **C**over and Concealment
- **O**bstacles
- **A**venues of Approach and Escape

Timber—any lumber, the least dimension of which is 5 inches or greater.

Truss—a rigid framework of wooden members (and sometimes metal bars) designed to support a floor or roof. They are designed as a series of triangles and usually manufactured off-site.

Turnaround Circle—the area between fixtures, appliances and/or walls necessary to comfortably use them. Often used in bathrooms to determine minimal size requirements, in which case a diameter of about five feet is considered ideal.

Vent Pattern—the distinctive combination of types, styles and locations of vents on a roof. Vent patterns are highly dependent upon floor plans and provide reliable clues to the walls underneath as well as identifying other structures with the same floor plan.

Window Group—two or more windows installed in such close proximity to one another that they function as a single window component. For diagramming purposes, a window group should be considered as a single window.

Work Triangle—the paths between the kitchen sink, stove and refrigerator. Normally this should be between 12 and 22 feet to ensure adequate space without a feeling of being cramped or constricted.

Appendix B: Diagramming Principles (Rules of Thumb)

The following heuristic rules are organized in the general order they appear in the book and/or are grouped together by subject. For example, all rules relating to vents, doors or windows are grouped together even if they were introduced in a different order.

Cardinal Rule of Contracting

The ability to overcome construction design difficulties is in direct proportion to the amount of money the builder is willing to spend.

Rule of 14

When the width of a house or wing of a house exceeds 14 feet; suspect the presence of an interior wall. The more the width exceeds 14 feet, the greater the likelihood of an interior wall.

45 Rule

Whenever you observe a roof with a pitch of 45° or greater, suspect the presence of a living space under the roof. This is almost always a sleeping area.

Cardinal Rule of Diagramming

As the number of details you use to predict the location of inside features increases, so does the degree of reliability and precision of your diagram.

Multiple Vent Rule

The more vents that project from a roof, the more likely it is that there is an interior wall directly beneath them.

Perimeter Vent Rule

When a roof vent is not in an exterior wall, the closer it is to the edge of the roof, the more likely it is that there is an interior wall beneath it.

Limited Option Rule

Vents extending (anywhere) through shed and flat roofs are strong indicators of an interior wall beneath them.

Vent Pattern Rule

Any pattern of vents, regardless of their style, type, purpose or combination, that is repeated on another building provides near conclusive evidence that the floor plans are identical.

Public Entry/Exit Doors

All public entry doors and all doors available to the public swing toward the outside of the building.

Exterior Residential Doors

All residential entry doors swing into the building and are not less than 36 inches wide or more than 48 inches on any one leaf.

Interior Door Rule

Generally, all interior doors swing into the room and against a wall.

Window Analysis Rule

The distance between a known wall and a window is equal to the distance between a suspected wall and the window.

Window Alignment Rule

With few exceptions, windows are installed from the top down (at the same height as a door—80 inches) and over one another.

W=2H Rule

When the width of the window is twice or more the height, it is almost always a bathroom window.

Dormer Window Rule

Windows in dormers or gables are strong indicators of living or sleeping areas above the first floor.

Window Group Rule

When the space between two or more windows is less than the known distance (K) treat the windows as a single component. Likewise, when a door swings toward an immediately adjacent window, both the door and the window are in the same room and should be treated as a single component (W).

Obscured Glass

When a window has obscured glass, suspect a bathroom.

Rectangle Rule

Because houses are constructed from a series of rectangular rooms, determining the length of any two adjacent walls in a room provides a reliable method for calculating the remaining two since the opposing walls must be the same. By repeating this method with other rooms, the entire shape of the house is revealed.

Mirror Rule

Separate dwellings in multiple-dwelling structures tend to use reverse floor plans, which are mirror images of those adjacent.

Intuitive Rule

Because houses and apartments have more similarities than differences, when in doubt use your own home for insight.

Appendix C: Useful Websites

In this day and age, websites provide an abundance of useful information for tactical diagramming. In researching this book, I found the following websites to be especially useful. They are organized by their general focus but listed in no particular order. With a few exceptions, I have included only those websites which provide the information for free.

Regional Information

http://www.ffiec.gov/geocode/default.htm—Provides demographical and census data for the neighborhood of a given address.

http://www.mapquest.com, http://maps.yahoo.com—Provides detailed street maps of a given location and driving directions between any two points.

http://maps.google.com—Provides not only maps but also satellite photos for many areas, as well as a hybrid configuration that identifies major roads on the satellite photo.

http://zip4.usps.com/zip4/welcome.jsp—U.S. Postal Service information on zip codes.

http://www.zip-codes.com/distance_calculator.asp—Find the distance between any two zip codes and/or all the zip codes within a given radius, includes latitude/longitude coordinates

Satellite Views

While not construction oriented, the following sites provide tactical diagramming advantages by providing a "birds-eye" view via commercial satellites. Care needs to be exercised, however, because the photographs vary from a few months to several years old and some require subscriptions.

http://earth.google.com—Combines 3D graphics and networks streaming to produce high quality images of earth, including "fly arounds." Provides an ability for navigation for convoys and tactical teams, including orientation from terrain features. (requires free download)

http://www.bing.com—This site allows 3D "fly arounds" using both aerial imagery and maps. The photographs are quite clear and navigation is exceptionally easy using just a mouse and the control key.

http://www.terraserver.com—This site is more of a "broker" in providing imagery from a number of providers. It has topographical maps and downloadable JPEG images with a resolution varying from 2 feet to 2 meters. Prices will differ depending on the image provider. Allows preview of images at 8 meter resolution.

General Residential Construction

http://www.nahb.org—National Association of Homebuilders home page. This site provides a wealth of information on every aspect of residential construction, including designs, materials, techniques, statistics, multi-family construction, books and other home building associations. As a "one stop shop" this site is a good place to begin searching the web for any diagramming question.

http://www.contractors.com—This site is designed to assist homebuilders and buyers and is maintained by a network of professional builders, architects, engineers and designers. Besides providing a wealth of useful building information, it provides well-organized links to other building information sites.

http://www.homerepair.about.com/homegarden/homerepair—This site provides detailed information from a variety of sources on many aspects of home building and maintenance, including code requirements and detailed diagrams for framing and the like. It is particularly useful for tactical diagramming because it is organized by subject with more than 700 links to subject specific topics.

http://www.bhg.com/home-improvement—The "House & Home" link on this page, maintained by *Better Homes and Gardens*, contains all kinds of information for designing kitchens, bathrooms and the like, and provides information on house plans and common appliances as well as landscaping security information.

http://doityourself.com—"Do it yourself," often abbreviated DIY, is almost an American way of life. This site provides a wealth of information useful for tactical diagramming. An additional advantage of this site is the large number of links to other, more specific sites, providing an organized "gateway" to a wealth of building information.

http://www.askthebuilder.com—This site is one of the best organized for quickly finding useful tactical diagramming information on the Internet. Besides being well organized, it provides a series of pull-down menus for quick access to building information of all kinds, and even videos on some subjects.

http://www.constructionweblinks.com—Maintained by a law firm (Thelen Reid & Priest LLP) specializing in construction-related law, this site provides a host of links to other building sites, including statistics, government regulations, building codes, public records, engineering and architectural information.

http://ebuild.com—This site provides one of the most comprehensive building information sites on the web. Information is intuitively organized in folders to allow users to quickly find building-related information, including house plans, appliances, hardware, landscape design and many others.

http://buildfind.com—One of the few search engines oriented specifically for the building trades, this site provides a wide category of useful diagramming information that is greatly enhanced by a user-defined search capability.

http://www.thebluebook.com—This site contains a database of more than 880,000 construction-related companies that are categorized by region and their specific line of business. The use of the database is free and can quickly provide tactical diagrammers building information specific to their individual questions and/or region of the country and individual needs.

Kitchens and Bathrooms

http://www.kitchen-bath.com—Provides information on kitchen and bathroom designs, including dimensions, minimum clearances, appliances and the like. (For bathrooms see http://www.kitchen-bath.com/bbasics.htm, and for kitchens see http://www.kitchen-bath.com/kbasics.htm)

http://www.nkba.org—Maintained by the National Kitchen and Bath Association, provides information on kitchen and bathroom designs, including dimensions, minimum clearances, appliances and the like.

Factory-Built Houses

http://www.modulartoday.com/modular-building-codes.html—This site explains many of the features in modular homes and includes links to the associated building codes for each state.

http://www.modularcouncil.org/mc—This site is maintained by the National Modular Housing Council. It is useful primarily because of the number of individual links to other websites focused on the design, installation and purchase of modular housing.

http://www.modularhomesnetwork.com/default.asp—This site is maintained by J.R. Consumer Resources, Inc., and Modular Homes Network and is focused on all things related to modular houses. It provides an ability to look up a number of features related to modular housing, including free reports and floor plans.

Drawing (Diagramming) Software

While there are a number of good Computer Assisted Drafting and Design (CADD) programs available, most have been designed for those intending to build a house, like architects, draftsmen, contractors, and so forth. While they are "full featured" they tend to be expensive, and difficult to learn and use. The following are three excellent CADD programs that are relatively cheap and easy to use.

http://sketchup.google.com/index.html—SketchUp is free software provided by on the World Wide Web by Google. It can be used to create 3D models of anything and is especially useful for tactical diagramming. It works with both Macintosh and Windows computers, is easy to learn and use, and provides an ability to quickly adjust the size of objects by stretching, hence the name focused on sketching rather than drawing or drafting. It has online video tutorials that are also free. Moreover, this program provides an ability to work from actual photographs to include measuring and drawing scale and adding features directly onto a photographic image. A more powerful version is available for purchase.

http://www.punchsoftware.com/index.htm—Punch Home Design software has a variety of modules specifically designed for users with no home design experience. It is easy to use and provides both 3D and 2D views, to include floor plans and blueprints. It provides an ability to conduct a virtual walk through and fly around view. The majority of the graphics in this book began using this program.

http://www.chiefarchitect.com—Chief Architect has software designed for both lay people and professional home designers. It has all the features of Punch software described previously. It also includes free online training videos. The standard defaults for the program are those most often used in the building industry. For example, "install-ing" windows in a wall automatically defaults them from the top down at 80 inches, which is by far the most common method when actually building them. The updates for this book were done using this program.

Appendix D: Tactical Diagramming—Step by Step

Nowhere in this book is a process required, or even suggested, for how to complete a reliable tactical diagram. Every tactical diagrammer tends to develop their own preferences and methodology. Notwithstanding, some procedures have proven so beneficial that they have become established as best practices. This appendix will describe a method using four steps that have consistently yielded reliable and accurate diagrams.

First, work from large to small.

Start with the orientation of how you want the diagram to appear on paper. For most, this will simply be using cardinal directions with north at the top of your diagram. Nearly as often, however, is when a target is on a north/south street and the front of the house (one side) is positioned so it faces the bottom of the diagram as if the viewer were approaching the house from the street. In either case, it is always beneficial to indicate north with an arrow.

Once the orientation has been chosen draw in the large and easily discernible features like fence lines, property lines and building outlines. Some diagrammers also choose to include major landscaping features, such as hills, creeks, trees, streets, curbs, sidewalks, and other immovable objects since they also assist in estimating proportions, distances and locations. Since most tactical diagrams are not to scale, only the perspective is important, but efforts to be precise early will pay off later.

Second, work from confidence to ambiguity.

This means to sketch in as many features that can be reliably placed and sized before moving to those that are less reliable or more difficult to determine. Entrance doors of houses, for one example, are nearly always visible and are almost always the same size (36 inches wide by 80 inches tall). Likewise, driveways, sidewalks, garage doors, masonry chimneys and other features are not only conspicuous but their sizes can be relatively easily determined or reliably estimated. As the diagram gains more and more detail many confusing aspects can be more easily and reliably determined.

After all the features that can be confidently placed and sized are drawn, begin working on those features that will affect interior floor plans, especially windows and vents. Windows are typically installed in the middle of interior walls in a room and so provide strong clues as to where interior walls are located and conversely, where they can't be. (see Chapter Nine) Similarly, vents are most often installed inside walls, which means they almost always terminate through the roof directly above them. (see Chapter Seven). After these features are placed it is much easier to estimate the location of the interior walls.

Third, continually compare.

This means to continually review your diagram as it gains details. As the diagram increases in detail it becomes easier to locate and estimate dimensions of rooms, closets and interior walls. Compare what you know or believe to what you can see. Be suspicious! Do not automatically discard incongruities but rather seek explanations. Don't be afraid to admit that you just don't know.

Last, with only one exception,

working on a diagram collectively rather than individually always produces better and more precise diagrams.

The knowledge and perspectives of more than one person provide knowledge, comprehension and insight beyond even the best individual effort. The single exception is when speed is more important than time, in which case some compromises must be made. Generally, this means that the diagram will have less detail and to some degree, less precision. At a minimum, however, a good tactical diagrammer should be able to quickly and accurately determine the three parts of a house, the precise location of the front door and the most likely location of the rear door, as well as many other useful features for planning and decision making.

Index

additions
  common types of, 143
  identifying, 144–45
  rules applied to, 144
  as wing, 145
adversaries, 24–25
affluent community, 3
air conditioning, 90–91
alleys, 39
alpha-numeric method, 33
altitude, 162
apartment buildings, 150–157, 151n19
appliances
  bathroom, 133
  technology and, 43

architectural features
  floor plans determined by, xv
  floor plans predicted by, 6, 154
  predictions made by, 6, 51, 119–20,
    115–21
  windows with, 112–113
attics, 73
  apartment buildings with, 151n19
  as room below roof, 64–74
avenues of approach and escape, 17, 18,
    163, 167

Baratta, Rick, 24n1
barriers, 17, 18, 177
base lines, 29
bathrooms
  bedrooms serviced by, 113
  corridor of, 134
  half-bath, 132
  in-line, 134
  information for, 190

L-shaped, 136
obscured glass in, 107
plumbing required by, 147
as smallest room, 132
smallest windows for, 108–109
soundproofing provided by, 133
venting for, 90
windows for, 110–11
beam, 54–56
bearing walls
  load supported by, 58–60
  ridgeline and, 64
bedrooms
  bathroom servicing, 113
  houses categorized by, 135–37
  styles of, 135–37
  windows for, 138n16
Bill of Rights, 48
breakfast nook, 129
building basics, 51–52
building codes
  bathroom requirements meeting, 132
  bathroom window requirements meet-
    ing, 90, 110–11, 132
  bedroom window requirements meet-
    ing, 138n16
  dimensions regulated by, 61
  doors/light switch relationship in, 102
  doors regulated by, 93–102
  fire safety provided by, 45
  first appearance of, 48
  food preparation area and, 53n2, 128
  inhabitable room requirements from,
    113–14
  nonmanipulative door locks required
    by, 95
  stairways regulated by, 147–48

building practices
 tactical diagramming facilitated by,
  105, 148–50
 windows and, 112, 113, 114–19
buildings
 construction knowledge for, 1
 elements controlled by, 52
 exit doors required by, 98
 gravity influencing, 44–45
 value considerations for, 27
bump-out additions, 144
burglar bars, 18n8
business
 exterior doors for, 94–95
 interior doors for, 98–101

camera
 digital photography with, 163–64
 drive-by photos from, 160–62
 fly-by photos from, 162–64
cardinal directions, 32, 166
cardinal rule of contracting, 56, 183
cardinal rule of diagramming, 65, 117,
  183
 features used for, 117
 inside features predicted by, 65–66
casement window, 109
ceiling joists, 59
channelized terrain, 25
chimney(s), 42, 61, 88, 113, 140, 152
city blocks, 30
civilian population, 26
closets
 bedrooms having, 137
 window analysis accounting for, 114,
  117–18
combustion vents
 as roof's largest, 87
 toxic vapors vented by, 85–89
communications, 25–26
compartmented terrain, 25
computers
 at home, 41, 43, 48, 138, 139
 CADD, 191
 reverse diagramming facilitated by,
  166
 tactical diagramming simplified by,
  174

concealment, 16, 177
condominiums
 diagramming rules applied to,
  151–52
 ownership style for, 151
construction industry
 apprenticeship for, xv
 building knowledge and, 1
 residential information for, 188–90
contracting, cardinal rule of, 56, 183
contractor, 152
corridor
 bathroom, 134
 cross-aisle terminating at, 157
cottage industry
 information age growing, 48
 work at home trend creating, 41
coup d' oeil, 177
 commander's ability from, 20
 as intuition, 19
cover and concealment, 15
Crip, 10

databases, 32
decentralized control, 26
decisive terrain, 13, 177
defensive advantage, 24
deployment, 35
detectives, 159–60
digital photography, 163–64
doors
 centered, 100
 exit, 98
 exterior business, 94–95
 exterior front, 94, 95, 97
 forcing open, 103n19
 garage, 102–4
 interior business, 98–101
 locks for, 101
 placement of, 93
 residence main entrance, 95–98
 sectional, 103
 swing direction for, 157n29
 tactical diagramming importance of,
  93
dormer window rule, 74, 185
dormers, 178
 gable, 74

as roof surface projections, 73–74,
   144
shed, 74, 75, 144
drain system, 79–80
drive-by photography, 160–62
drugs, 4
ducts, 89. *See also* vents
duplexes
   reverse floor plans in, 152
   tactical diagramming difficult for,
      151
   two or more dwellings in, 150–51
dwellings
   detached garages converted to, 104
   duplexes as, 150

eaves, 76
economic influences, 46–48
environmental influences, 44–46
exit diagram, 99
exterior residential door rule, 97, 184

factory-built homes
   diagramming identical for, 170
   identifying, 171
   information for, 190
family room
   as busiest room, 138
   tactical diagramming for, 139–40
features, nearly useless, 76–77
fields of fire, 9, 12, 13, 15, 178
film speed, 161, 163
fire
   floor plans impacted by, 45
   harm coming from, 15–16
fire codes, 105, 157
fire escapes
   fire codes requiring, 157
   tactical diagram assisted by, 100
fireplaces
   as zero-clearance, 42
   as zero-tolerance, 88–89
flashing
   roof jack type, 89
   vents using, 81
flat roofs
   limited option rule for, 84
   outlying buildings using, 68, 69

floor plans
   architectural features determining,
      xv
   architectural features predicting,
      152
   bearing walls predicting, 61
   fire impacting, 45
   house sectioned for, 52–54
   individual dwelling conventions for,
      155–56
   innovations influencing, 42
   knowledge of, 6
   people interviewed about, 167
   rectangles arranged for, 125
   vents determining, 77, 79
   zoning ordinances impacting, 50
food preparation area, 53, 107, 111, 128
45 Rule, 64, 183
foyer, 97, 139, 140
french doors, 98n10
furnaces, 87

galley kitchen, 129
gambrel (barn) roofs
   dwellings using, 69
   large spaces using, 69
garage doors, 102–4
garages
   detached, 102, 104
   as standard additions, 47
   tactical diagramming simple for,
      102
glass
   bathrooms obscured, 107
   light reflected by, 106
gravity, 44–45
great depression, 47
greenhouse windows, 107n4
"gunslingers," 4

half-bath, 132
header, 55
headroom, 69, 73
hip roof, 68, 69
home design, 44
home office, 43
homeowner's association, 153–54
horizontal beams, 55–56

hotels, 147n9, 149n16, 149, 150, 151, 155
house(s)
  age of, 112
  bedrooms categorizing, 135–37
  bedrooms' location in, 137–38
  door primary entrance of, 95–96
  financial worth reflected in, 46
  furnace centrally located in, 87
  influences on, 37–38
  living rooms in, 138–40
  as mini-environment, 44
  notebook sketch of, 4
  occupant averages for, 40
  old, 148
  parts of, 52–54
  rectangles making up, 125
  rooms determined for, 125
  row, 46, 150
  sections of, 52–54
  size increasing for, 41
  smaller more popular for, 39
  tactical diagramming examining, 120
housing design, 48
housing market, 47

information age, 47
interior door rule, 101, 184
interior walls
  multiple vent rule indicating, 83
  perimeter vent rule locating, 84
  roofs locating, 63
  skylights not over, 75
  water appliance vents indicating, 81,
    82, 83, 91, 118, 120, 147
interviews, 167
intuition, 19
intuitive rule, 127, 185

Jefferson, Thomas, 28
judgment, 20

key terrain, 177
  avenue of approach and escape from, 18
  control advantage from, 12
kitchen
  bedroom windows different from, 111
  breakfast nook in, 128
  configurations of, 125–31

in-line, 131
information for, 181, 190
L-shaped, galley, 128, 130
U-shaped, 127, 129
water heater near, 86
KOCOA, 12

lighting, direct, 27
limited option rule, 84, 178
living area, 52–53, 61
living room
  older houses with, 138–39
  tactical diagramming for, 139–40
living space, 64
loads
  rafters distributing, 65
  walls bearing, 58–60
local ordinances, 49
log cabins, 57
louver window, 109

mansard (French) roofs, 71, 72
map, 21
master bedroom, 136–37
materials, roof, 72
meridians (range lines), 29
metes and bounds, 28
micro-terrain, 21, 178
minor rooms, 140–41
mirror rule, 155, 185
mobile home, 171–72
modular method, 170
monitor roofs, 70–71
motels, 147n9, 149n16, 150, 151n21
movement
  sniper reporting, 36
  tactical numbering system describing,
    35
multi-story houses, 39
multiple-apartment building
  multiple-dwelling zoning for, 151
  tactical diagrams of, 155
multiple dwellings, 88, 150–57
multiple-story buildings, 33–35
multiple vent rule, 83, 180

narcotics warrant, 3
navigational system, 32–36

negotiators, 160
North Pole, 29n7
notebook sketch, 4
numbering system. *See* tactical numbering
    system

obscured glass rule, 107n3, 179
observation, 175
    concealment preventing, 16
    as suspect surveillance, 13
obstacle, 17, 18, 177
orientation, 35

panelized method, 170–71
panic locks, 95
pantry, 141
partitions, 59, 60– 61
passage locks, 101
pedestrian door, 103
perimeter vent rule, 84, 184
photography
    drive-by, 160–62
    surveillance examining, 112, 119,
        123
    tactical diagramming using, 159–62
photography, fly-by
    L-shaped flight path for, 164–65
    methods for, 162–66
pitch, 178
pocket doors, 101
police officer, xiv
political influence, 48–50
post and lintel, 54
    horizontal/vertical framing members
        in, 54, 56
    as simplest construction method, 55
post–World War II era, 47
privacy locks, 101
prominent terrain, 170, 179
    as easily identified, 20–21
    search narrowed by, 161, 166
property, 28
property boundaries, 33
public entry/exit rule, 95, 184
public land survey system, 28–29

rafters, 179
    load distributed by, 65

roofs supported by, 64
range lines (meridians), 29
rectangle rule, 125, 185
reflections, 106
remodeling
    bump-out additions for, 144
    reconstruction from, 38
    tactical diagram and, 60, 72
residential information, 188–90
reverse diagramming, 179
    computer facilitating, 167
    interviews used for, 167
    for rooms/buildings, 166
reverse engineering, 51
reverse floor plan
    appearances changed for, 156
    floor plan model for, 155
ridgeline, 64
roofs
    additions pitch different for, 146n4
    combustion vents on, 87
    dormer projections from, 73–74
    gable, 67
    gambrel (barn), 69–70
    hip, 68, 69
    interior walls located with, 63, 75, 83, 84
    mansard (French), 71, 72
    materials covering, 72
    monitor, 70–71
    rafters supporting, 64
    styles of, 66–72
    water appliance vents small for, 79–80
rooms
    addition type of, 143–44
    bathroom most frequently used, 132
    rectangles determining, 125
    size of, 45, 61
    sun, 146
rule of 14, 60, 179, 183
Rybczynski, Witold, 38n1

satellite information, 162, 187
sectional doors, 103
sector of fire, 15, 179
shadows, 81
shed roofs
    limited option rule for, 84
    outlying buildings using, 68, 69

single-family homes, 50, 149, 150,
     152n23, 153, 154
skylights, 74–75
slab doors, 103
sleeping area, 53, 54
sniper, 36
social climate, 40
sociological influences, 38–41
solar heating panels, 76
span, 179
stack vent system, 82–83, 180
staircase, outside, 148
stairways, 147–49
stick framing, 57, 58
stories, upper, 146–49
stove vents, 89–90
street addresses, 29–30
street gang, 10
street signs
     different color/style for, 30
     different jurisdictions for, 31
structural insulated panels (SIPs), 171
stud, 180
subdivision, 29
sun rooms, 146
surveillance
     photographs examined for, 112, 119,
          123
     suspect observation as, 13
     tactical intelligence from, 108
survivalist, 14
suspect
     negotiators dealing with, 160
     surveillance of, 13
     weakness for, 19
SWAT operations, xvi, 3
swinging doors, 101, 102, 137, 141

tactical diagram(s)
     fire escape plans assisting, 100
     house influences on, 37–38
     house sections contiguous for, 53–54
     kitchen important to, 86
     micro-terrain always on, 21
     multiple-apartment building with, 155
     perspective absent in, 126
     remodeling important for, 72
     reverse engineering similar to, 51

tactical diagrammer, novice, 7
tactical diagramming
     bathroom door/window location for,
          133
     building practices facilitating, 148–49
     classes taught in, xv
     condominiums/townhouses rules for,
          152–55
     doors important to, 93
     duplex building practices with, 150
     duplexes difficult for, 150
     factory-built homes with, 170
     features useless for, 76–77
     garages simple for, 103
     helpful aids for, 157
     house insides examined by, 120
     information from, 6
     intelligence obtained from, 159
     kitchen important in, 127
     living room with, 138–40
     minor rooms and, 140
     old houses challenge for, 151
     other countries similar for, 173
     photographic information for, 160
     precision less from, 116
     regional information for, 187
     satellite information for, 187
     SWAT operations using, xvi, 3
     as terrain analysis extension, 20
     tools necessary for, 174
     upper stories complicating, 146–49
     windows used in, 105
tactical information
     alpha-numeric method providing, 33
     surveillance providing, 108
tactical numbering system
     as navigational aid, 34
     as navigational system, 32–36
tactical objective, 17–18
tactical operations
     attics used in, 73
     compartmented terrain influencing, 25
     coordinating component of, 28
     drive-by photography planning for,
          161
     terrain analysis impact for, 12
     terrain influencing, 9
tactical planning, 23

tactical teams, 35
technology
    appliances and, 43
    house design influenced by, 41–43
terrain. *See* also key terrain; urban terrain
    field of fire influenced by, 15
    micro-, 21, 178
    tactical operations influenced by, 9
terrain analysis, 180
    field of fire considered in, 15
    fundamentals same for, 23
    key features identified by, 10
    tactical diagramming extension of, 20
    tactical operation impact from, 12
three-dimensional quality, 24
timber, 57, 173, 180
timber frame construction, 57
toilets, 133
townhouses, 150
    common sidewalls connecting,
        153–54
    diagramming rules applied to, 153–54
    regulation of, 154
tracts, 28–29
trailer parks, 172
trusses, 180
    rooms larger because of, 42
    strength/popularity of, 66
    as triangular shaped wooden frames,
        64–65

Uniform Building Code (International
    Conference of Building offi-
    cials), 48
urban environment, 26–27
urban terrain
    characteristics of, 23–27
    influence of, 10
    navigating, 27–28
U.S. Constitution, 48

vapors, 85–89
vent pattern rule, 91, 92, 184
vent rules, 84
ventilation, 111, 135
vents
    bathrooms with, 90
    exhaust vapors removed by, 85–89

flashing used for, 81
floor plans determined by, 77, 79
interior wall indicated by, 83
Vietnam, xiv

walk-in closets, 133n13, 136, 137, 140,
    141
walls
    as load-bearing, 58–60
    types of, 58–61
    wet, 136
water
    buildings influenced by, 45
    heater, 85, 86
water appliance vents
    interior walls indicated by, 83, 91,
        118, 120
    locating, 147
    precise location determined by,
        162–63
    as roof's smallest, 80
    window analysis using, 118–20
water heater, 85, 86
weapon, 15
weapon coverage, 13–15
wet wall, 136
W=2H rule, 111n7, 185
Whitman, Charles, 13
wind, 45
window(s)
    analysis example for, 114–121
    building practices for, 105–14
    grouping of, 121–23
    information gained from, 106
    large, 112
    looking through, 105–8
    medium-sized, 111–12
    shapes of, 113
    size indicators of, 108
    small, 108–11
    styles of, 110
    tactical diagramming using, 105
window alignment rule, 59, 146, 184
window alignment, 59, 109, 144–45, 146,
    147
window analysis
    adjustments to, 122
    building practices and, 114–19

window analysis (*continued*)
    closets accounted for in, 117–18
    complex, 119
    formula for, 115, 116
    rooms predicted by, 117
    rule for, 114–15, 184
wood frame construction, 56–58
work triangle, 128, 181

zip codes, 30–32
zoning categories, 49–50
zoning codes, 172
zoning laws, 49
zoning ordinance
    building construction type from,
      48–49
    floor plans impacted by, 50

Tactical Diagramming Training
Materials for Instructors (CD)

$20
UPC 7-93573-93765-0

An essential companion CD for teachers of tactical diagramming.
Materials include a suggested course outline, lesson plans,
PowerPoint slides, and student handouts.

Available from www.lanternbooks.com.